NATIVE GHOST STORIES

Darren Zenko & Amos Gideon

LONE
PINE

Lone Pine Publishing International

The Publisher: Lone Pine Publishing International
Distributed by Lone Pine Publishing
1808 B Street NW, Suite 140
Auburn, WA 98001
USA

Websites: www.lonepinepublishing.com
www.ghostbooks.net

National Library of Canada Cataloguing in Publication Data

Zenko, Darren, 1974–
    Native ghost stories / Darren Zenko, Amos Gideon.

    ISBN-13: 978-1-894877-76-3
    ISBN-10: 1-894877-76-4

    1. Ghosts--Canada. 2. Ghosts--United States. 3. Indians
of North America--Folklore. 4. Ghost stories, Canadian (English)
5. Ghost stories, American. I. Gideon, Amos, 1975– II. Title.

E98.F6Z46 2006   398.2089'97   C2006-903784-1

We acknowledge the financial support of the Government of Canada through the Canada Book Fund (CBF) for our publishing activities.

 Canadian   Patrimoine
Heritage   canadien

PC: P33

For The Storytellers

Contents

Introduction 6

Part I: Stories by Darren Zenko

The Return of Only Daughter 10
The Man Who Was Afraid of Nothing 29
Heavy Collar and the Ghost Woman 38
The Legend of White Horse Plains 65
Blue Jay Goes to Ghost Town 73
Chase of the Severed Head 103

Part II: Stories by Amos Gideon

Bad Son and the Spider Woman 130
Multnomah Falls 146
The Skull 153
Thunder Without A Storm 165
The Empty Village 193
The Madness of Mocking Crow 198

Introduction

Ghost stories are universal. They are universal because death—and the hope and fear of what may come after death—is universal, and stories of ghosts and the spirit world give humans a means of dealing with that final certainty. Like all cultures around the world and throughout time, the native peoples of North America have developed a rich, diverse and valuable body of ghost and spirit lore.

The idea of a single thing called "Native culture" is about as valuable as the idea of a single "European culture"—the grouping does nothing to reflect the diversity of individual peoples within the group. There are many similarities, and shared cultural elements, but the way in which a Chinookan of the Northwest approaches life will be very different from that of a Hopi of Arizona.

The way in which he approaches the afterlife will be different, too. Ghost stories, in North America as elsewhere, are very concerned with issues of social propriety, ritual observance and cultural taboos: consider the stereotypical Hollywood horror movie, in which teenagers who violate social norms by drinking and having sex are punished by a supernatural monster. Ghost stories, like all stories, transmit elements of the culture that creates them; there's much to be learned by studying a people's approach to the dead and the not-quite dead.

My stories have been adapted into a modern fiction style, while at the same time being as faithful as possible to the original source material. I hope that in these stories you can catch a glimpse of the depth and breadth of the cultures of our continent's first people, and that you're inspired to explore further.

Of course ghost stories are also meant to entertain, so I also hope that you enjoy yourself in these pages. Keep a fire burning…and watch where you sleep.

Darren Zenko
Edmonton
June 2006

Part I:
Stories by Darren Zenko

The Return of Only Daughter

Here's a story of a journey to and from the world of the dead, but in this case we stay firmly in the world of the living and watch as a dead girl returns to life. As with many stories, the focus here is on the necessity of playing by the rules of the spirit world when dealing with ghosts; in this case, the hunter does everything right and his medicine effectively midwifes the dead girl through her rebirth. There are greater forces at work, though; the spirit world demands sacrifice in return for violating the natural order, and the resurrected girl and those who love her pay the price, not only for her return to life but for her earlier bucking of the social norm of marriage.

Like many peoples, North American and otherwise, the Sioux traditionally practiced platform burial. Four stout timbers, seven or eight feet tall, would be erected and a bed about 10 feet long would be built between them. The body was prepared with sacred medicine and wrapped in layers of blankets and fine robes, so tightly as to be waterproof, and laid on the bed—raised off the ground, it would not be dug up and devoured by scavengers. Offerings of food and drink—sustenance for the spirit of the deceased—were hung in baskets from the scaffold.

This story is adapted from "The Resuscitation of the Only Daughter" in McLaughlin's Myths and Legends of the Sioux.

The old woman knelt on the robe-covered floor of her lodge, listening to her dying daughter's labored breathing, thick with the bubbling sound of life's waters running wrong. The girl's face, which once shone with life and captured the hearts of many young men, was drawn and pale, slick with sweat; eyes that once sparkled rolled behind half-closed lids, unseeing. None of her mother's skill in healing had brought relief, and no medicine or prayer offered by any medicine man could stop the advance of the sickness. Only five days had passed since the girl had taken ill, and she lay now at the doorway to death.

So early in dying, the girl had been late in arriving. Her mother and father had been childless for many years, and such was their love that her father had never taken another wife, though many of his relations had urged him to do so. Childless, they lived their lonely life until, at a time in life when most would be doting over grandchildren, their most fervent prayers had been answered with a swelling of the woman's belly. Despite her age, the bearing was easy; when winter had passed through spring into summer, they held in their arms a beautiful baby girl.

When the time came for her naming, she came to be called Only Daughter—the old couple and their relations knew there would be no more children after her. In her their hopes rested, with dreams of a good marriage to a skilled man, perhaps even grandchildren should they be blessed to live so long. But as the baby girl grew into a young woman, those dreams receded. Many young men, hunters and war-riors, courted the beautiful and talented girl and sought her for a wife, but always her answer was no. Neither pleading or threats from her mother and father nor gifts and declarations of love from the young men of the tribe could move her. She was fixed on a single life and wanted no man.

And now there would be no more courting, no more hunters bringing gifts, no more youthful warriors boasting and dancing in the hope of catching her elusive heart. Even now, the timber for her gravesite was being prepared. Miles from the camp, on a platform raised above the reach of wolves and bears, her body, wrapped in the finest blankets and fur robes, would be laid on a bed of willows and brush. Her mother and father would cut their hair and tear their clothes to rags, and all their horses and furs and fine possessions would be given away to others. Destitute, they would mourn. The loss of the things of this world was nothing; all they loved was already being taken from them.

The girl's congested breathing lost its deathly rhythm, becoming a shallow, ragged pant, then a rattle, then silence. Into that silence the old woman wailed.

*   *   *

Two years after the young woman's death, a man of her tribe and his wife were returning to their people from a long hunting trip. The man had dreamed well, and they'd been fortunate—loaded down as they were with meat and furs, they could not ride very fast. In silence they passed the place where Only Daughter's weathered and sagging funeral scaffold stood—it wasn't wise to speak in a place like that. About a half-mile further on, they decided to camp for the night.

Their campsite was a bit too close to the burial place for the hunter's comfort—he had been well taught by his grandfather in the ways of such things—but they were weary from riding, and the place they'd found was ideal. A clear and sparkling spring burst from a cleft rock, creating a bubbling little stream, and along the stream's banks the grass was green and sweet smelling in the air of early evening. With sighs of relief, the hunter and his wife dismounted, tethering their horses in place to drink and graze before setting up the small lodge they used when traveling.

The sun had long since gone down by the time the couple settled down inside their little tent for their evening meal. The smell of fresh deer meat and good wild vegetables stewing was more than welcome at the end of a long day of travel. But just as they were about to tuck into the simple, hearty dish, the hunter's dogs began to bark and howl outside the tent. At first the hunter assumed some animal was passing nearby and the dogs would subside after they'd scared it away with their noise, but the snarling and growling continued for a long time.

"Look out the door and see what it is those mutts are barking at," said the man to his wife. The wife pulled back the tent flap and looked out into the moonlit night. When she drew her head back into the tent, her face was pale and her eyes were wide with fear.

"There's...there's something that looks like a w-woman out there, coming from the direction of that girl's funeral scaffold! It's...it's..."

"Yes," replied the husband, completing his wife's terrified thought, "it's probably the ghost of the dead girl." He tried to keep his voice steady, though his heart was pounding, his skin crawling. His grandfather had made him familiar with the ways of medicine and the spirit world, though the young man had never taken a medicine man's initiation, and he knew much of the precise etiquette required when dealing with ghosts. "We must let her come, and must not act as if we are afraid."

This was easily said, but not so easily done. The young couple sat still as stones and faced each other across the glowing coals of their little cook-fire, barely daring to breathe as they listened hard to the sounds of the night. Even the barking of the frantic dogs turned to whimpers, then cowed silence as the thing approached. Now, the couple could hear soft footsteps on the grass approaching with a painfully slow tread. Step by step they came closer, whispering through the grass until they came to a stop right outside the door of the tent. The hunter forced himself to look down at the narrow gap between the door flap and the ground, and there he saw a small pair of moccasins. His guest had arrived.

He looked up at his trembling wife, and her eyes, as they met his, were brimming with tears of terror. Through the lump in his throat, he struggled to find his voice. At last, he managed to squeak out: "Please come in, whoever you are, and have something to eat."

They couldn't bring themselves to look at the door; they heard the sound of the heavy hide cover as it was pulled from the portal, the shuffle of moccasined feet, a creak and rustle as their eerie visitor settled herself on the blankets covering the floor of the little lodge. They could smell her now, too, a pungent aroma of rich earth, weathered hides and medicine herbs mingling with the wholesome scent of the simmering stew. She sat in silence. The hunter found the courage to turn his head to regard their guest.

The figure kneeling there in the red light of the cook-fire was still wrapped in her grave-clothes. The robe that bound her from head to toe was once of highest quality, a treasured possession, but had since been turned mottled black by time and weather. It was still tight to her body, covering her head, her hands, her face. Nothing of her long-dead flesh could be seen beneath that moldering shroud, and the hunter was thankful to be spared the sight.

Looking back to his wife, he made a quick gesture with his head toward the robe-wrapped figure. With shaking hands the living woman dished out a steaming bowl of the simple food she'd prepared and set it in front of her guest. "P-please," she squeaked out, not daring to be impolite, "you...must, must be hungry. Eat, my friend."

The shrouded figure did not take the bowl, nor did it uncover itself to eat. Like the corpse it was, it sat still and unmoving in the dim light.

"Let us...let us give our guest some privacy," the hunter said, "and turn away so she may eat." This they did, the hunter filling and lighting his pipe, smoking in silence while his wife made herself desperately busy; with clumsy, trembling fingers, she scraped sinew from the deer's bones for later use as thread. Behind them they heard the whisper of hide on fabric as their guest pulled away her shroud, followed by the gobbling, smacking sounds of a starving person tucking into food for the first time in a very long time.

It wasn't long before the sounds of eating stopped, and the hunter's wife felt something bump against the sole of her foot. Reaching behind her without looking, the woman felt the now-empty bowl. After washing up the vessel, which had practically been scoured clean by their hungry visitor, the woman and her husband turned back toward the thing in the doorway. The robe was once again tightly wrapped around the figure's face, and it sat unmoving as before; it didn't even make the tiny motions of a breathing creature.

After a long moment, the hunter's curiosity and his grandfather's teachings compelled him to speak. "Are you," he asked, boldly, "the young girl who, two years ago, was placed upon that scaffold?"

With a slow, slow movement like a tree rocking in a light wind, the figure nodded once, twice, three times. The hunter thought he could hear the scraping of dead joints from inside the weatherworn shroud.

Though he was afraid of what the answer to his next question might be, his people's customs of hospitality and his fear of offending a thing of the spirit world bid him to speak again: "Are you...will you stay with us here, tonight? M-my wife will make a bed down for you." He heard his wife stifle a wail in her throat before it could reach her mouth.

With a dry rasp of bone on bone, the dead girl's dark, shrouded head turned agonizingly from side to side. The young man's wife made another tiny sound, like a wordless prayer of thanks; he flashed her a stern glance of warning.

Remembering what his father's father had told him about the ways and habits of the dead and how they never visited a man but once, the hunter asked his third question: "Will you be coming again to see us tomorrow night?"

Again, the thing in the doorway gave its slow, bowing nod.

"Well...well, then," the man replied, "it is good. We will see you tomorrow night. You are welcome with us."

The man and his wife watched as the dead girl's withered muscles slowly pulled her creaking, cracking body to its feet. The ghost pushed past the door covering and shuffled back into the darkness beyond, back toward the gravesite from which it had come. The stunned couple sat in the failing light of their hearth, listening to the slow, steady swishing of dead feet receding through the damp grass until the night was once again silent.

*   *   *

Three nights the shade of the dead girl visited their little camp beside the stream, taking a meal in silence and going back the way she came. The hunter's wife at first begged that they might pack up and leave, flee back to their people, but he wouldn't allow it. When dealing with the world of spirits, he knew one must follow spirit laws to the letter. He shuddered to think what might happen were they to give offense to their ghostly visitor. So each day they waited in camp for their nightly guest, hardly daring to look in the direction of the funeral platform. While the woman tried to keep her mind occupied with what busywork was available in their makeshift traveling camp, the young man could do nothing but smoke, think and toss stones in the stream—hunting or trapping would mean leaving his terrified wife behind in that haunted place.

The third night began like the others: the wild barking of the hunting dogs, then silence, then the ponderous whisper of dead feet through the damp-night grass, then the visitor at their door. But on this night, once the undead thing had eaten its fill, the hunter noticed a new thing—the dead girl was breathing! At first he thought it must be a trick of the flickering firelight, but as he looked closer at the shrouded figure, trying not to stare and perhaps give offense, he was sure of it: the wrapped corpse's chest was rising and falling in lifelike rhythm, and the wheezing of shallow breaths could be heard over the popping of the dry sticks in the hearth.

There was something else, too. A fold of the girl's moldy funeral robe had come loose, exposing one of her hands. The skin was shiny and pure black, drawn tight against the bone since the underlying flesh had shriveled and shrunk like dried meat. Seeing this, the hunter had an idea. Taking his medicine bag from the pole on which it hung, he began rummaging for the ingredients he needed. He could feel the shrouded being watching him along with his wife as he ground and pounded special roots along with skunk oil and vermillion. He knew this as a strong medicine against burns and diseases of the flesh. If human food could bring the breath back to the dead girl's body, then maybe...

"Friend," the hunter said when the medicine was ready, "if you will let me rub this medicine on your hands and face, it will bring the life back to your skin. It will put flesh on you, and bring back your complexion. Will you let me do this?"

The shrouded corpse nodded in its usual slow way, though the hunter fancied that he felt a certain eagerness in the way the dark and weather-stained cowl dipped and rose. Steeling his stomach, the young man reached out and took the dead girl's blackened, skeletal arm in his hands. How brittle it was, how delicate! The fingers of the hands were like twigs in a drought, as if they would snap at a touch. With great care he rubbed his medicine into the hard, dry skin and repeated the treatment on the other limb, softly singing a song of healing. The musty, earthy smell of the walking corpse rose up around him and mixed with the pungent aroma of the hunter's medicine.

When the girl's hands and forearms had been treated, he moved on to the hidden face. He didn't look at what he was doing; he didn't dare look. He just reached through the folds of the shroud and rubbed in the medicine, singing his song. But even though he couldn't see the dead face, he could feel it under his hands: tight dead skin stretched across the high cheekbones, scraps of ragged cartilage where there was once a nose, a lip-less mouth filled with loose teeth and deep, empty sockets where eyes had withered away. Everything in him moaned with revulsion, but the wise, young man filled his mind and heart with the power of his medicine, and soon the deed was done.

Arms once again folded into the depths of the burial robe, the dead girl rose from her place on the floor and went noiselessly out into the night, back toward her resting place on the platform in the woods. Even after she had gone, the odor of the grave and the reek of the medicine lingered in the close air of the little traveling lodge. The weary couple knew they hadn't seen the last of their bizarre guest. Sighing, the hunter lit his pipe and let the good, sweet smoke chase the bad smells up and out the smoke-hole.

The morning of the next day was spent moving their camp a few miles closer to the village—the couple knew their guest would follow them—and in the afternoon they set about replenishing a supply of ingredients for the hunter's special salve. If his belief in the power of that medicine was true, he'd be needing more of it that evening. His wife, still very frightened and wanting desperately to be gone and back to their people, would not let him out of her sight. As they searched for the plants the hunter needed, she asked him in a whisper, as if the dead girl miles away could hear her: "Is it good, what you're doing? Bringing a dead person back into the living?"

Her husband didn't pause in his digging of roots, though in fact he had asked himself this same question many times that day. With a confidence that he didn't feel, he replied, "I am not bringing her back to life. She brought herself back, or some power brought her. Either way, I do what I must, because to do otherwise would bring disaster to me. It is good."

"Yes," his wife replied without much conviction, "it is good."

Heralded by the usual chorus of frenzied dogs barking, their visitor that night was obviously changed from what she had been. Still wrapped head to toe in dank black hides and ragged blankets, the walking corpse moved now more naturally, with less stiffness. The shroud over her skull was no longer pulled so tight; though it still hid the thing's face completely, it now hung more like a heavy veil than a mask. When the dead girl entered the couple's tent and knelt in the guest's place, her movements were almost elegant.

As she had the three nights previously, the hunter's wife offered a bowl of steaming stew to the resurrected girl. But before she could place it on the blanket in front of the dark figure, the girl's hands came forth from her wrappings and received the bowl as a living guest would. The hunter and his wife were amazed to see the girl's hands, which, though pale, were now fleshed out and natural-looking. But still she would not eat until the couple had turned away.

When the girl had finished and had once again wrapped herself completely, the hunter addressed her. "My medicine, did it help you?" The girl nodded, gracefully now. "Do you want my medicine rubbed all over your body?" The shroud dipped in assent. "Very well," said the hunter, "I will make enough to cover you entirely, and then I will go outside, while my wife puts the medicine on you."

At this, his wife gave a strangled cry and stared at her husband with wide, frantic eyes pleading *no*. He stared back with a hard look that let it be known she was to obey. Taking down his medicine bag, he mixed his salve in silence. When he'd made up a large enough quantity to cover a person head to toe, front to back, he handed the container to his wife, who hesitantly took it with trembling hands, and left the tent without speaking. Outside, he sang his medicine song and stared at the stars for a long time, until he heard a tapping on the wall of the tent.

When he pulled back the hide flap over the doorway, the stench of grave dust and skunk oil struck him like a blow to the face. Fighting not to retch, he staggered inside and took his place. His undead guest was once again wrapped tightly in her burial clothes, and his wife knelt in her place, staring unseeing at the floor, with her body trembling and her eyes brimming with tears.

"Tomorrow—" the young man began, before a cough cut his words off; the air in the tent was beyond foul. Recovering, he continued: "Tomorrow, we will travel and reach our village. Will you travel with us?"

The dead girl shook her head, *no.*

"As you wish. Will you come again to our tent tomorrow night, after we have camped in the village?"

A nod, *yes.*

"Do you want to see your parents, then?"

With another almost-graceful nod, the not-dead girl rose to her feet and left the tent as silently as she came. When she'd gone, the hunter took out his pipe and smoked furiously to clear the small space of the stink that filled it. He looked over at his wife, who still knelt as she had when he'd entered, shaking and staring at the floor, silently crying.

"You are a strong woman," he said. "You did well."

His wife did not move or reply, only dropped tears at her knees.

*   *   *

The young hunter sat in his big lodge in the camp of his people. Its cover was good hide and its poles were straight and strong; his robes and blankets were warm and comfortable, and a fine home-fire burned in the hearth. *I should be comfortable, now,* he thought, thinking of how he'd like to be calling his friends and relations over for feasts to celebrate his successful hunting trip, *but I have to see this through.* He'd broken camp very early in the morning and traveled as quickly as possible to reach the village. On their arrival, he'd immediately sent his wife to the shabby little lodge of the grieving old couple in order to inform them of what had happened. Sunset was approaching; he expected the dead girl's parents at any moment.

As if in echo of his thoughts, he heard at that moment the sound of someone approaching his doorway and call out a quiet greeting. It was the old man and his wife, and the hunter invited them in. They sat in the places of honor and received the good food that his wife had prepared with some grace, but their troubles hung heavy about them. Their mourning had not been easy; here in the firelight, the hunter could see the depths to which grief had gouged the natural lines of age, pulling their features into a mask of hopelessness. Their clothes were torn and dirty, *they may well be the same clothes they ripped to rags the day their daughter died,* the young man thought, and though their bodies must have been crying out for the feast before them, they only nibbled as much as politeness required. Dazed and apprehensive, the heartbroken couple waited for the hunter to explain the bizarre story his frightened wife had earlier stumbled through.

Just as they had finished eating, or pretending to eat, there came a great noise from the entire camp. Every dog in the place, it seemed, had started up barking and howling at once, filling the night with the sounds of their fear. The old couple exchanged wide-eyed glances, not understanding what kind of animal could create such frenzy in the village dogs, but the hunter held up a hand for calm. He knew that the dogs would fall into frightened silence when the dead girl entered the camp itself. When that happened, the sudden quiet seeming almost as loud as the barks, he spoke at last to his guests.

"Your daughter who was lost is coming now, to rejoin the living. Be brave, and you will soon see her." The old woman held her face in her hands; the old man just stared, bewildered.

They heard the sound of feet approach the doorway and stop, waiting. The sticks in the fire popped and crackled. Taking a deep breath, the hunter called out: "Come in, and be welcome."

The door was pushed aside, and the shrouded figure ducked and entered silently as always, taking a seat in the lodge with smooth, natural motions. The burial clothes were no longer wrapped so tightly around her body but hung loosely like a robe, and the dark hide that once closely covered her face now covered her head almost casually. The smell of death, too, was gone; there was only the odor of the mildewed shroud and the hunter's medicine. Hands and arms pink and healthy as a prairie rose came forth from those dank folds and reached upwards. Taking hold of the two sides of that worm-eaten hide, the hands pulled the shroud away from the girl's head and let it drop away.

There stood revealed the beautiful young girl who had inflamed the desires and captured the hearts of so many young men. Her skin was pale from having not seen the sun, but it glowed from within with life and health. Black eyes with pinpoints of firelight in them shone out from above her delicately carved cheekbones. Her nose was straight and noble, her mouth a ripe summer berry. Cascades of glossy hair tumbled in a wild dark rush over her shoulders, still tangled with scraps of the rawhide thong that had bound her braids at her funeral. The hunter had never seen a girl so alive.

"Mother, Father," she said, breaking the stunned silence with a cool, clear voice. "I have returned."

Shrieking, the old woman flung herself at her miraculously returned daughter, almost scattering the fire as she did so. The girl's father wasn't far behind, and the two old people, so long lost in their two years' worth of grief, were now in a frenzied embrace, kissing and hugging the girl, rejoicing. The sound of their joy carried out into the village, where word had spread of what had happened to the hunter in the woods, and the people marveled at the wonder of Only Daughter's return.

At long last, after nearly smothering their daughter, the old couple subsided and sat beaming in their places around the hunter's hearth. Their happiness had in one moment taken the trouble from their eyes, while the joy flooding their faces turned the deep canyons of their grief into lines of laughter. Even the hunter's wife, who had so recently been horrified by the thing the returned girl had been, watched the scene with eyes gleaming. Only Daughter sat calmly and returned their happy looks with a gentle smile. The hunter himself had at first been puzzled by the girl's calm, but now he began to understand. The way back from death to life must be a hard road; in the girl's eyes was the look of one who has seen much, of wisdom gained at a high price.

"Well...well," said the old woman, fluttering her hands in front of her, looking around at the people in the lodge as if searching for something. "What...what now? I don't even know what's supposed to happen, now. Will you come back home with us, daughter?" When she spoke, the hope that rose up in her eyes was heartbreaking.

"No, mother," said the girl, soothingly. "My time in your arms has long since passed. I once made the mistake of wanting to stay always a girl, and I won't make it again. No, my place is here, with the man who brought me back into the living." With this, she looked over at the hunter.

"Huh!" her father snorted in surprise, though he could not have been so surprised as the young hunter. "I had always hoped you'd marry, but this is... Ai! My head is spinning! Well...well, what do you say, young man? Will you take my daughter to be your wife? I have no dowry, as you know..."

The hunter did not know what to say. He was too young to be thinking about a second wife, but this...this was different. What should he say? What should he do? His grandfather had never said anything in his lessons on the ways of the spirits about taking a wife that had returned from the dead. Was he still bound by the rules of the spirit world? Would he *always* be bound by the spirit world? He looked once again at the beautiful young girl sitting in his lodge and decided it might not be so bad to be so bound.

"Hm! It is good, Grandfather," the hunter replied. "Your daughter is treasure enough. I will take her as my wife." The girl's mother once again began to cry with joy, while the hunter's good-natured first wife smiled a genuine smile of welcome; macabre though the girl's arrival had been, she knew enough to appreciate a miracle.

"And now," said the young man, beginning to relax for the first time in many days, "I think it is time to call a big feast. There is much to celebrate tonight."

*   *   *

Only Daughter lay in her lodge and thought about that night; she was an old woman herself, now, and yet that night was as clear to her as if it had just happened. She remembered the feeling, like waking from a deep sleep, as her hands had pulled her shroud away from her face. She remembered looking into the young hunter's face and knowing it was destiny that she'd stay with him. She remembered the shouting and the laughter, and the awe of her people when they saw her alive and walking once again. She remembered tasting good food as if for the first time. Smiling at the memories, she tried to laugh, but the coughing, the waters of death, had already entered her ancient body.

When the thick, wet coughing had finally subsided, she reached for her pipe and lit a bowl of medicine she knew couldn't keep her alive much longer. Yes, that had been a good night, the night she came back to the living and found her husband. He was the finest of her men, her wise hunter—it had been a bitterly tragic time a year later, when she learned he had been lost while riding to war, that his strong young legs would never again carry him through the forest after game.

The smoke calmed her breathing, allowed her head to clear and memories to rise. She married again soon after the death of her first husband; this man had clever hands and a laughing tongue. He, too, went away to war and didn't come back, chasing after an enemy raiding party that had stolen some of the people's best horses. She was still beautiful then, and it wasn't long before she had another suitor, a warrior of great renown. His list of daring deeds had come to a conclusion soon after they'd married, when he died at war from a coward's arrow. After that, no more young men came after her hand—the people now considered her holy, and believed that any man who took her as his wife would soon be dead.

So she gave her life over to tending the sick. The ways of medicine came easily to her, and she did things without thinking that many medicine men took all their lives to learn. She gained a reputation as the greatest healer of her nation, and with her talents, she held many people back from traveling too early to that dark place she'd once visited.

She wondered about that place now, as she listened to her own body struggling to take in air, as she heard her own heart failing. She had no memory of being dead. What was the world of the dead like? What had she done there? She looked over at the neat bundle by the door to her lodge, the finest of the many fine robes she owned. *Ah, well,* she thought as she struggled out from under her blankets and on to her feet, *time to find out.*

The effort of standing brought on the coughing once more, and once more after it had passed, she lit her pipe and took in great clouds of the sweet smoke that had saved so many lives. It only had to keep her breathing for a short time more; she hadn't far to go. She reached down for the robe on the floor and wrapped it around herself, singing a medicine song. When she was ready, she called out to one of the young men who waited outside her lodge. The boy entered and she leaned on his shoulder. She didn't need him to guide her; she could feel the pull of the place she was going to. She could have walked there with her eyes closed.

The platform still stood in a little stand of trees near where a spring gushed forth to water the sweet grass. It had been repaired at her direction and made ready for her. Many hands helped her up to that bed of fine ash boughs.

She pulled the robe and the blankets tight around her.

She reached up and fixed the shroud firmly over her face.

Once more she went into that deep slumber, never again to return.

The Man Who Was
Afraid of Nothing

Not all ghost stories are frightening tales of hauntings or accounts of harrowing journeys into the underworld. In almost all cultures around the world, humorous ghost stories serve the purpose of allowing people to deal with death and dying— through these stories, the fear and horror surrounding death and the dead becomes something that can be coped with, even laughed at. In teasing and tormenting the ghosts he encounters—and casually handling their bones—the fearless hero of this story turns death into a laughingstock, much as the Chinook prankster Blue Jay does when he visits the ghost town (p. 73), though with happier results.

This story originates with the Brule Sioux of South Dakota, and was told by the storyteller Lame Deer to ethnographer Richard Erdoes. I have adapted it from the version that appears in American Indian Myths and Legends.

So, these four ghosts are sitting around one dark winter's midnight, having a good time, when...

What? You don't think ghosts can have a good time? Of course they can. They have fun in their own way, and they remember some of the things they liked when they were alive. These four ghosts mostly remembered three good things:

smoking, bragging and gambling. That's how they would spend their nights.

OK, as I was saying, these four ghosts are sitting around one winter's night, talking, smoking ghost smoke and having about as good a time as ghosts can. One of the ghosts says, "I heard some men talking while I was out haunting near here a while ago. Apparently, there's a young man around here who's not afraid of anything. He's not even afraid of us, so these men said."

A second ghost, perched on a rotted old log, snorts with derision: "Not afraid of us? Huh! I bet *I* could scare him."

The third ghost is indignant. "Well, we ought to teach this punk kid a lesson. It's a matter of ghostly pride. It's our duty to make him scream and turn his hair white and leave him crying for his mother."

The fourth ghost rubs its ghost hands together, throwing off little sparks. "How about we make a bet on it, boys? We go out there and give it to him good, and whoever spooks him the most, wins."

Well, all the ghosts are pretty bored by that point, having all been dead for quite some time, so the idea of a wager sounds exciting. So they all agree to bet their ghost horses, the only property of any value in the ghost world.

So the first ghost goes out to wait by a trail where it knows this supposedly fearless man will pass by. It doesn't matter how long it waited there. Ghosts don't really care about time. Eventually, the ghost sees a man approach and right away it knows it's him. This guy's got kind of a crazy look in his eyes, and he's grinning and singing to himself, just walking along without a care even though he's passing through a place where people have been seeing ghosts. The ghost thinks that maybe the guy's simpleminded.

The waiting ghost jumps out in front of the smiling man. It's taken on the form of a skeleton, which it figures is just about the scariest thing there is. "*Hou,* friend!" the ghost shrieks, and starts clacking its teeth together. The sound echoes in his empty skull and makes a sound like a war drum.

"*Hou,* cousin," the man replies calmly. "I'd love to talk with you, but I have to be going. Could you please step out of the road so I can pass?"

This isn't going the way the ghost had planned it. It thought that it would have won those ghost horses right away, with the teeth-chattering. It'd always been proud of its scary teeth. It doesn't give up, though. "No!" it shouts, making its voice like a howling wind. "You may not pass until we have played the hoop-and-stick game! If you lose, I'll make you into a skeleton like mee*eeeEEE!*"

That last shriek wasn't for spooky effect. The ghost was wailing because the fearless man had grabbed it by the wrists and ankles and bent its skeleton body into a big loop, tying it off with some prairie grass! "Well, here's the hoop...where's the stick?" he asks, laughing. "Ah! Here it is!" And with that, he grabs one of the skeleton's leg bones.

"Here we go!" the man shouts, and starts rolling the moaning and screaming skeleton along the path, scoring over and over again by putting the stick through the speeding hoop until the poor ghost hits a rock and tumbles to the ground in a whimpering pile of bones.

"Well, looks like I won that game," says the smiling young man, catching his breath. "What game are we going to play now?" He looks down at the scattered bones. "I know!" he says, "how 'bout a little field hockey?" and he starts swinging the leg bone and driving the ghost's skull ahead of him like a ball.

"Oooww!" the ghost screams, "Stop! Stop! You're giving me a headache! You're killing me! Owwww!"

"You're already dead, friend," the man replies. "And besides, who proposed we play games, huh? You or me? You're a pretty silly ghost." And with that, he winds up and swings that bone, knocking the howling skull away in the night. Leaving the ghost's bones behind, he keeps on walking.

Pretty soon, he comes up to where the second ghost is waiting. Now this second ghost, you know, it figures it's pretty clever—it wasn't killed yesterday. It knows how to scare a man, and it wants those ghost horses pretty badly. So it's taken the scariest form it can think of—the form of a skeleton—and when the fearless man walks by it jumps out and grabs at him.

"Let's dance, friend!" it wails in its best ghost voice, wrapping its bony arms around its victim.

"Hey, that's a good idea, cousin ghost," the young man replies, ducking out from under the ghost-skeleton's embrace. "But how can we dance without music, huh? What are we going to use for a drum and a drumstick?" The man makes a big show of looking around for something suitable before his eyes light up.

"I know just the thing!" he cries, and before the startled ghost can say or do anything he reaches out and snatches the skeleton's skull and thighbone and begins dancing around, singing while beating on the skull with the bone.

"Oww! OWW! Stop! This is no way to dance," the ghost cries. "You're hurting me! Stop it!"

"What are you talking about, you lying ghost?" the young man asks, annoyed. "Everybody knows ghosts can't feel pain."

"I don't know about other ghosts," says the skull in the man's hand, "but me, I'm hurting."

"Huh! I didn't know ghosts could be so sensitive," the man replies. "You really disappoint me. Here I am, just getting into things and having a good time, dancing and singing some good songs, and you ruin everything by being a crybaby. Well, go do your whining somewhere else!" And with that, he hauls back his arm and flings the skull over a hill, then scatters all the ghost's other bones in different directions.

"Oh, now look what you've done," comes the ghost's complaining voice from the other side of the hill. "It'll take me ages to get all my bones back together. You're a jerk."

"Ah, you should thank me," says the young man as he walks away down the dark trail. "It'll give you something to do."

So this fearless fellow is continuing on his way when, in the moonlight, he sees a pale figure up ahead, blocking the path. Sure enough, it's the third ghost in the form of a skeleton. "This is getting monotonous," he thinks to himself as he approaches the bony spirit.

"*Hou*, friend ghost," the young man calls out. "Didn't I meet you before, a ways back up the trail. You look mighty familiar."

"Nah...those were my cousins," the ghost replies. "They're wimps, but I'm tough!" The ghost makes a motion like it's flexing its muscles, forgetting that there's no meat on its bones. "Let's wrestle. When I win, I'll turn you into a skeleton like me!"

The man thinks about that for a second, then replies, "Hmmm...you know, if it's all the same to you, I really don't feel like wrestling. What I'm really in the mood for is a bit of sledding. There's more than enough snow on this hill here to make for some really good runs. But what can I use as a sled? What I really ought to have is a couple long buffalo ribs, but... Aha!" Before the tough ghost can do anything, the fearless man has reached out and yanked away the skeleton's rib cage, running with it up the hill.

"Wheee! Oh, this is fun!" he cries as he zips down the hill on the borrowed rack of bones. "You really ought to try it!"

"Stop! Stop!" the ghost wails from the bottom of the slope. "You're breaking my ribs! Oh, please stop that!"

The young man glides to a stop, laughing. "Friend, please don't be insulted, but you look so funny without your ribs." He's laughing even harder now. "I mean, look at yourself! You're so short, with your head resting on your hips. What a funny trick!"

"Come on," whines the ghost, "give them back. They're the only ribs I've got!"

"You want them? Then go dive for them," the young man says, laughing, as he flings the rib cage into a cold creek running nearby.

"Hey, now that's not nice." The ghost stands there, pouting. "What am I supposed to do without my ribs? How am I going to show my face at ghost meetings looking like this?"

"Well, just jump in the water and swim for them," the man replies. "I must say, you do look as though you could use a bath. It'll do you a world of good, and I'm sure your woman will appreciate it."

"What? What are you talking about?" the ghost shrieks. "I *am* a woman!"

"Oh, my apologies, you pretty thing," the man says, walking away from the fuming ghost. "With skeletons, it's so hard to tell."

The young man continues on his way for a while, humming to himself and enjoying the crisp, clear winter air. Soon, a wind starts to blow up from the north with a eerie howling, and there in front of him appears the fourth ghost, who was a powerful chief in life, riding upon his ghost horse—a skeleton riding a skeleton.

"Foolish man!" the skeleton chief calls out, his voice like rolling thunder. "I have come to kill you!"

"Skeletons again?" asks the fearless man, annoyed. "What is it with you ghosts and skeletons? You really need to broaden your repertoire if you're going to make a go of scaring folks."

"What...what are you talking about?" the ghost replies, shocked at the man's nonchalance. "Skeletons are scary. Everybody's scared of skeletons."

"No way, cousin. Skeletons are old-fashioned. Even little kids aren't scared of skeletons these days. Take it from me... I'm a ghost myself!"

The young man starts making horrible faces at the ghost. He pulls his lips back and bares his teeth, foaming at the mouth. He waves his arms in the air and howls, shaking his head and stomping his feet. He rolls his eyes back until just the whites are showing and screams like a wounded animal. The ghost chief starts to get scared, then, thinking this young man really is a powerful ghost, and begins to wheel his horse away in order to escape.

The fearless young man reaches up and grabs the glowing bridle of the skeleton horse, stopping it in its tracks. "A horse is just what I want," the young man shouts. "I've walked enough for one night!" Pulling on the skeleton's bony legs, he yanks that scared old ghost chief right out of his ghost saddle and flings him to the ground, scattering his bones. The young man can still hear that spirit whimpering as he rides off into the night.

So, let me tell you something, there's not much that runs or flies that's faster than a ghost pony. That young fellow has the ride of his life that night, leaping over forests and hills, speeding across the prairie, laughing all the way. And almost as soon as he started his ride, he's back in the camp of his people, laughing and shouting and riding that horse all around. Well, everybody in the camp gets scared then, running into their tipis and peeking out as the fearless young man has his fun. It's getting close to sunrise by this point, though, and as soon as the sun sends its first bit of light over the horizon, the ghost horse vanishes into mist, dumping the laughing young man right down on his behind.

Everybody comes out of their lodges, then, eager to hear the fellow's story. He's already a hero in his camp for being so fearless, but riding a ghost horse? That pretty much tops anything he's ever done. So they gather around and the young man tells them all the story of the four ghosts he met, and how he got the better of them all.

"Wow!" says one man. "You really are fearless!" "Yeah," says another, "you're definitely the bravest guy around. I'd follow you anytime." All the other men present nod and agree that the fearless young man is going to be a great leader. Then one fellow looks at the brave young man and points at his arm.

"Hey, cousin, what's that there on your sleeve?"

The man who was afraid of nothing looks down at his arm, and there, staring back at him with eight black legs, is the most awful, hideous creature he's ever seen, a fat black body and creepy hairy legs, with huge jaws like two big knives. And then he screams. He starts screaming like a baby.

"EEEEEEE! Get it off! Get it off me! Aaagh! Help! Somebody! Hellllp!" He's crying and shaking, his pounding heart about to jump right out of his chest. He's writhing on the ground.

At last somebody comes to his rescue—a young girl, his brother's daughter. Laughing, the child plucks the little spider from the brave warrior's sleeve and tosses it away into the bush.

Heavy Collar and the Ghost Woman

A horror of skeletons, as the physical remains of the dead, is pervasive throughout Native culture. Ghosts are most often described as animated skeletons, and there are countless harrowing tales of luckless travellers who've had the misfortune of coming in contact with bones that have been improperly laid to rest.

One major theme among these stories is the idea of a road-weary man unknowingly sleeping next to the skeleton of a dead woman, and waking up to find himself haunted and hounded by his new ghost-wife.

This Blackfoot legend set somewhere in the semi-arid grasslands shared by Montana and Alberta is one such story, based on an account published in George Bird Grinnel's 1892 classic, Blackfoot Lodge Tales.

His breath came in ragged gasps; his chest ached from exertion. He was a brave man, a hunter and warrior of the Kainah, the Blood tribe. He'd led men to war and counted coup many times, earning honor and respect, and he'd never run from anyone or anything in his life. But he ran now, headlong through the night, stumbling in exhaustion, the noise of his breathing and his passage through the grass as loud as thunder on the still prairie.

He knew what he was doing was foolish. The enemy was nearby, and the land was bright as day under the nearly full moon in the clear, late-summer sky. Hostile scouts could spot him out in the open, making so much noise. He should have been down in the coulees and depressions, moving silently, watching and listening, a shadow. And yet, he ran—the thing behind him was more fearsome than any bullet or arrow, knife or hatchet.

Luck was not with him. His toe caught a prairie-dog hole, and he stumbled face-first to the ground. He lacked the strength to get up; all he could do was lay there gasping. The thing behind him drew closer every moment, but he could not move. His heart felt like it would burst. He prayed for deliverance, gulping air. When the fire in his chest had burned itself down, he forced his breathing to a shallow rasp and tried to listen to the night.

The sighing of the wind over the grass was all he heard, and for a moment he dared to imagine he'd outrun the horror that had chased him. But then it came, the swishing sound of someone in the distance hurrying through the dry grass, and a woman's terrible voice howling his name in rage and despair: "Ooooooh, Heavy Collar! You dog! You've killed me, Heavy Collar...you've killed me again!"

A fresh surge of terror rushed through him and he lurched to his feet, staggering on through the night. Clouded by fatigue, his delirious mind wandered as his body ran on, taking him back to the day his nightmare began...

*　　*　　*

It had been a luckless hunting trip. The young leader had collected seven men and headed out from the Blood camp on the river, leading them deep into the hills in search of buffalo. For days they searched in vain for game. The animals had likely been frightened off by a large war party that had passed through the area. The possibility of meeting this hostile group made the young chief lead his hunting party with caution through ravines and low places, further reducing their ability to spot the scarce game.

Oh well, thought Heavy Collar as he moved carefully along the bank of the river, *it's still another two days back to camp. Maybe we'll have some luck yet.*

He was scouting ahead of his party for animals and enemies. The sun, dropping into the west, was tinting the sky with the colors of the approaching autumn. Heavy Collar was about to turn back to rejoin his men for the night when he rounded a bend in the river and spotted three big old buffalo bulls on a steep bank, heading down to the water. The hunter cut over into a dry gully to circle silently around the animals. Slowly he crept up, and when he was in range he took careful aim with his bow—with enemies around, he didn't want to fire his rifle—and dropped the fattest buffalo with a single arrow.

Heavy Collar trotted up to his kill while its companions scampered away. It wasn't the youngest, most tender meat he could have wished for, but the animal had been strong and healthy. He butchered it on the spot. Since he was hungry he took a nice piece for himself and went back into the gully, where he built a smokeless fire on the stony, scrub-covered floor as dusk came on. As he roasted the juicy meat, the warrior began to talk aloud to keep himself company, as he often did when camping alone.

"Huh. I should have waited for my men to catch up to me before going after those buffalo," he said as the meat sizzled on the spit. "They don't know I'm in this gulch. Maybe I should climb up and try to signal them before it's dark. I should get some buffalo hair and clean my gun while I'm at it."

Just then, a small movement caught the hunter's sharp eyes, and he turned to see a ball of buffalo hair, just the size he needed, come over the rim of the ravine and land at his feet. It seemed that it had floated in the air as if carried by an unseen person, but Heavy Collar dismissed that thought. A brief shiver of panic ran through him; some enemies might have sneaked up, heard him talking and tossed the buffalo hair at him as a taunt. He froze, listening.

He was surrounded by the sound of evening insects and birds, the whisper of wind, the faint rush of the nearby river. Somewhere, far off, a buffalo dropped its immense weight into a dust-wallow. But there were no rustlings in the grass, no whispers, nothing human or animal nearby. Still, he waited silently until the daylight was almost gone. Shrugging nervously, he picked up the clump of buffalo hair, wiped out his weapon and reloaded it. He was still very uneasy, listening hard in the gathering darkness. The stars were coming out, the moon rising. Deciding to scout out the country some more, he wolfed down the rest of his meal and kicked out his little fire. Back at the riverbank, he stalked warily downstream for a time. When it was very late and he'd reached the mouth of the river, the tired young man crawled into a stand of grass to sleep.

The very moment Heavy Collar fell asleep, he was jolted awake by the piercing sound of a woman's scream, jagged with terror. The sound came from very near, almost right on top of him. Listening hard, wide-eyed, the warrior lay unmoving, his heart pounding in his grassy hiding place, waiting for another sound. There was nothing but the night sounds of the prairie, sounds he'd grown up with, but now everything seemed strange, even malicious, as if dark spirits gathered just outside his sight and hearing, waiting for him to drop his guard so they could...what? Heavy Collar was too nerve-wracked to guess; he could only pray to every good and helpful spirit he could think of for strength and deliverance. By the time the moon had passed from the sky, exhaustion conquered fear and the man plunged into unconsciousness.

In that sleep, Heavy Collar found no rest. Foul dreams, swirling like the dreams of a man in the grip of a fever, filled his mind. There were flashes of frightened faces and glimpses of bloodthirsty marauders dressed in unfamiliar war gear. Once more he heard that heart-freezing scream, and along with it came visions of blood and murder—a grotesque, shouting mask of a face; an arrow finding its mark in an old woman's back; the features of a child twisted in a howl of terror. Monstrous whoops and war cries made evil music with groans and shrieks. And through it all, over and over, a vision of a young girl cut down by a knife across her belly, dying in slow agony as all around her friends and relations were slaughtered. After an eternity trapped in this nightmare, Heavy Collar at last came swimming like a half-drowned man back up to the waking world.

His eyes snapped open to the first light of dawn. He had sweated during his nightmare, and he was clammy and chilled, his joints and muscles sore. The dream-girl's screams rang in his ears, though the details of the dream, with its terrible power and foul omens, were fading. To have such an evil dream at home in his lodge would be bad. Plans for hunting or war would be put off, and he would seek cleansing medicine from a shaman or wise woman, like his mother back at the village. His mother would know what to do; she was renowned among all the people for the power of her exorcisms. But to have this dream so far from home, with enemies around, was the worst possible luck.

I'll be dead before I see my people again, Heavy Collar thought. There was no other way he could interpret his vision of death and pain. *At least those weren't my relations I saw in my dream. I didn't dream the deaths of my own people.* Worried, he began to stretch his cold and aching body. *If I'm going to die, I'm not going to die in a thicket like a wounded dog.*

Something brittle gave way under his right hand. For a just a moment he thought it was a bit of dry wood, until he saw the rest of it: beside him in the grass lay a human skeleton. Heavy Collar leaped to his feet with a cry. Getting a grip on himself, he inspected the bones. They were old and bleached; it was strange they hadn't been scattered by coyotes. But complete it was, laying there just as it fell, the bright white skeleton of a girl, the skull cracked by a blow from an ax.

Shuddering, Heavy Collar regarded the girl's bones and the matted patch of grass where he'd slept. They'd lain together as close as man and wife, he and that skeleton. Like lovers, her lidless eyes and lipless mouth close enough to kiss, his strong legs of warm flesh stretched alongside her brittle old sticks. He'd rested one night where she rested forever.

Heavy Collar shook his head. His thoughts were spinning in circles. He had to get out of this poisonous place. His men would be waiting for him at the buttes beyond the river, where they'd agreed to meet. Once back at his people's camp, he could get some medicine to clean the darkness of this place from him. Turning away from the bones in the grass, he started running, working the night's stiffness from his joints and praying for the rising sun to warm his soul as it warmed his body.

But he couldn't keep thoughts of the night's events from creeping into his head. He meant to be alert to the land, watching for enemies and game, but often he moved without seeing the country at all. A 20-man war party could have passed this way, or a large group of antelope, and Heavy Collar would not have noticed the signs, so afflicted was he with visions of himself and the murdered girl's skeleton sleeping together in that grassy bed. Sometimes he heard in the wind the screams he'd heard in his dream. He couldn't get them out of his head.

He traveled fast all day with no rest; his hard pace combined with plaguing, unhealthy thoughts wore him out before the sun had set. There were still many hours of travel left in the day, but when Heavy Collar came to the broad shallows of the river he decided to camp right there, on a little gravel island out in midstream.

A big fallen tree was beached on one end of the island, and it made a natural shelter against the wind. Heavy Collar made a small fire and sat down on one of the tree's old limbs with his back to the fire, trying to get warm; he'd been cold all day, even as he ran.

He thought about the night before: the dry gully, the ball of buffalo hair, the scream, the nightmare, the murdered girl and the skeleton he'd slept with. He felt haunted, cursed. He didn't know what to do. Heavy Collar worried that he'd lose his mind if he spent another night and day as he just had, thinking about that girl.

A sudden sound came from behind him, unmistakably loud over the babble of the river. It was a scraping, roaring sound, like a piece of lodge covering being dragged along behind his back on the gravel of the little island. It was the loudest thing Heavy Collar had ever heard; it filled his ears and set his hair on end, but he was so frightened, he couldn't even turn and look at what was making the sound. Closer it came, closer, until it sounded like it was right across the little fire from his back. It sounded like a bear's roar. Then it stopped. Now there was just the dry crackle of driftwood and the rush of the river. Heavy Collar prayed. The worst, he knew, was coming.

After a minute, which felt as long as a season, a new sound filled the air. It was a woman's whistling, impossibly high and sweet. Heavy Collar didn't recognize the tune, if it even had one, but it felt like a simple, soothing lullaby— a sound of home and happiness. To hear it coming out of nowhere there in the sunset wilderness was beyond unnerving, but Heavy Collar still had not moved from where he sat. He could feel the fire going cold at his back.

Slowly, the whistling changed. The tune became more sophisticated, like a song a young woman would sing when she knew a young man was listening. It sounded playful, beckoning...but then the low notes went weirdly flat and the high notes shrilled. It became a mocking thing, a parody of a love song. It sounded more like a dare; rather than being playful, it was a cruel tease. Desperate, the exhausted hunter at last made himself turn to look across the fire.

His heart almost stopped. There on the branch across from him sat the same bleached-white skeleton he had slept beside the night before, its grinning mouth opening and closing slightly as it whistled without lips. Around its shoulders was a half-rotted, dirty old tipi cover, riddled with holes, fastened at the bony throat with a knotted lodge-pole string. The lodge covering stretched back behind the skeleton and seemed to fade as it trailed into the distance. As the skeleton whistled its ghoulish song it kicked its dangling legs in time. Even without eyes in the shadowed sockets of its skull, the skeleton seemed to give Heavy Collar a lovesick stare.

Heavy Collar knew he would never have peace unless he could drive away this dark thing. He had no charms or medicine to exorcise spirits, so he gathered the tatters of his courage and spoke directly in the firmest, steadiest tone he could manage: "Oh, ghost! Please, go away and do not trouble me! I am very tired, and I need to rest and sleep. Please, leave me be!"

At Heavy Collar's pleas, the skeleton only whistled louder and harder, its song rising to a frantic screech to drown out the hunter's words. The more he begged the harsher its whistling became. The skeleton kicked its legs ever more violently, until the weathered old bones were beating savage time against the dry branch. It began to roll its head, looking left and right, up at the dusky sky and down at the fire, but always glaring back at Heavy Collar with its empty orbits.

Deprived of sleep, footsore from travel, hungry and haunted, Heavy Collar reached the end of his tether. Anger pushed fear aside as he stood up and shouted, "Fine! You won't leave me alone, no matter how much I beg you? Here, then, if I have to shoot you to drive you away, that's how it will be." With that, he snatched up his loaded rifle, threw it to his shoulder and fired point-blank into the middle of the rattling, whistling, horrible skull.

The report of the gun cracked the air and the fragile skeleton was blown off its perch, its ratty old lodge-cover robe swirling as it tumbled backward. The whistling stopped, and

Heavy Collar was about to look behind the big branch when a new sound took its place. A howling screech, a woman's voice echoing with a rage born of despair and betrayal, came from all around him. For the first time, Heavy Collar heard the voice of the ghost woman.

"*Ohhh, Heavy Collar! You dog! You son of a dog! You've shot me! You've killed me, Heavy Collar! My curse is on you! Do you hear me? There is nowhere you can run where I will not find you. You will never escape! You dog, there is no place you can hide! Ohh, Heavy Collar! You have killed me!*"

Clutching his gun, Heavy Collar dashed away, splashing through the river and up the opposite bank with the curses of the ghost woman howling at his back. He didn't know where he was running; he didn't know anything. His mind was nothing but a flame of fear. His feet barely touched the ground as he ran. The ghost woman's voice filled the sky, red with the setting sun: "*Heavy Collar, dog! I was killed once and you killed me again! Curse you, Heavy Collar!*"

Night fell and the voice of the ghost woman faded behind him, but still Heavy Collar ran on, too terrified to stop for even a minute. No matter how far and fast he ran, if he stopped to catch his breath he could hear that horrible accusing moan coming across the prairie behind him, calling his name and cursing him. His legs pumped and his lungs burned and his heart beat like it would burst. Grasses whipped his sweating body and the half-clouded moon bathed him in shifting light as he ran. The ghost woman was always right behind him.

By the time first light broke over the eastern horizon, his body had had enough. As the day brightened, his vision darkened, and he collapsed to the ground and slept where he fell. It was dreamless and deep—a sleep of exhaustion. He might have slept the sun around right there on the open grassland, had he not been roused before sunset by a cry that was by now horribly familiar. With heaven and earth echoing with curses against his name, Heavy Collar gathered himself and ran on.

*   *   *

Lying on his back in the grass, a young man watched the clouds tumble and shift, passing the hours while he waited for Heavy Collar to return. He listened to the sounds around him. The click and rattle was Lame Dog cleaning, checking and reloading his gun for the fifth or sixth time that day. Of the seven men who'd gone on Heavy Collar's expedition, only Lame Dog, Red Deer and Big Feather, who was off keeping lookout, had stayed behind to meet their leader. They were in friendly territory here, and in the two days since Heavy Collar had separated from them they'd had better luck hunting; the other hunters had gone back to their camp with the meat. For the three remaining men, there wasn't much to do but wait.

"Where could he be?" Lame Dog wondered, also for the fifth or sixth time that day. The energetic Lame Dog, tree-tall and weasel-nervous, wasn't very good at waiting patiently, a fault that often hurt his luck in hunting.

"Oh, he could be anywhere, Lame Dog," Red Deer drawled. "Maybe he was seduced by a mermaid and he's gone to live with the Underwater People."

"That's not funny!" The lanky Blood was very serious on the subject of spirits and the supernatural. "He could be hurt, or captured, or..."

"And what if he is?" Red Deer replied. "What can we do? Go out and look for him all over the land? If he's dead, it's out of our hands. If he's alive, he'll be here soon and we can all go home. Go set snares or something, keep your hands busy. Unless your gun barrel needs to be wiped again."

Lame Dog only grunted in response, and Red Deer heard him poking aimlessly at the fire. Red Deer shared his friend's worries; he'd known Heavy Collar all his life, and going off like this was unlike him. They'd found the buffalo Heavy Collar had killed and his little camp in the dry gully, but none of it made sense. Heavy Collar had taken no more than a small amount of the big old bison's meat. The fire in the camp had been allowed to die out. Nowhere near it were any signs that the warrior had spent the night. There was no blood, no sign of enemies or fighting; no one could pick up their leader's trail beyond the sandy riverbank.

A whoop from up on the ridge caught the two men's attention. Big Feather was waving for them to join him there. Red Deer got up and followed Lame Dog, who was already trotting uphill, gun in hand.

It was windy up there, and the view extended a great distance across country. Big Feather was a singularly ugly man, and one of his legs was shorter than the other, but he had the sharpest eyes of anyone around; he'd been quite angry with himself when he hadn't been able to pick up Heavy Collar's trail.

He was happy now, though. "Look over there!" he crowed, gesturing toward a group of distant hills. Though it was late in the day, Red Deer could make out a tiny speck moving down the face of a ridge.

Lame Dog squinted hard. "Is that a man? He's moving fast."

"Yeah, it's a man," Big Feather replied. "And he's moving fast, all right. He's practically falling down that hill. Oh, wait... he *has* fallen down that hill."

Red Deer couldn't see as well as Big Feather, but he did see a little dot on the hillside come to a stop. "What's happening?"

Now Big Feather was squinting. "Ummm...it looks like he's just lying there. Maybe he's hurt, or maybe he's catching his breath. If he was in that much of a hurry, he's probably been running all day."

"Is it Heavy Collar?" Concern for his missing friend and eagerness to be getting back to his lodge mixed in Lame Dog's voice.

"Can't tell. Hey, wait! There's someone else coming over the top of that hill. Not moving as fast, just steady."

Red Deer watched this new speck move down the slope at an unhurried pace. When it was part way down the hill, the first speck started moving again.

"Okay, our man's on his feet and running," Big Feather reported. "I think he's in rough shape, really tired. Why isn't he waiting for the other man?"

"Maybe he's being chased?"

"If he's being chased, whoever's chasing him doesn't seem to be in any rush to close the distance. He's just walking along as if he's...hey! I think it's a woman!"

"A woman? Are you sure?" Suddenly, Red Deer felt just as anxious as Lame Dog to go home.

"Pretty sure." As the hunters watched, the trailing speck reached the bottom of the hill, a few minutes behind their leader. "We're going to lose sight of them in that depression, but they're headed right this way. When the running man tops that rise, I'll be able to tell if it's Heavy Collar or not."

A long time passed before a figure came over the crest of the hill. Red Deer could now see that it was indeed a man, and that he was stumbling, running ragged. Big Feather, as usual, saw more and let out a joyful little laugh.

"It's him! It's Heavy Collar. Ai! He doesn't look so good."

The man on the hill once again staggered and dropped to the ground. Cupping his hands around his mouth, Red Deer shouted across the grassland. The man didn't move. Again, Red Deer shouted. This time the man lifted his head, and his arm came up in a wave before dropping back to the dirt. After a long time, Red Deer saw his body jerk, and the man pushed himself up off the ground with a spasmic thrust of his arms. Weaving like a wounded man, he ran across the face of the hill and disappeared into a deep ravine. A short while later the woman appeared and likewise vanished into the little valley.

"That ravine will take him almost right to our meeting-place," said Big Feather, turning away from the broad view. "We won't see him again from here. Can you believe it?" The misshapen warrior grinned. "No luck hunting, but he goes off and manages to take a woman. That crazy Heavy Collar!"

"Ah, what does he want with another wife? He's not that big a man, yet."

Red Deer didn't join in their bantering. "If he captured that woman," he said quietly, still looking thoughtfully across the hills, "why is he running away from her?"

Big Feather grinned. "Ha! Maybe she's left her people to follow Heavy Collar, sick with longing."

Lame Dog finished his companion's joke: "Yeah! And Heavy Collar's running away because she's old and ugly." The lean warrior twisted his face and body into a caricature that had the other man laughing.

"Ugly she may be," Big Feather countered, "but I don't think she's old. You saw her move; that was a real strong woman!" The two men headed down the back of the ridge.

Red Deer hadn't stopped gazing at the point where Heavy Collar and the woman disappeared into the ravine. Something was wrong. He turned away from the edge of the bluff and followed the other men to prepare for Heavy Collar's arrival and whatever trouble he was bringing with him.

When Heavy Collar dragged himself into camp a short while later, he was in worse shape than his men had expected. His body was damp with sweat and two days' worth of trail dirt that covered him in gray-brown grime. His skin was marked all over by small bruises, his knees were skinned, his legs and thighs striated by the red marks of careless passage through brush and bramble. His moccasins were nearly destroyed, and his feet were bleeding. Sunken deep in their dirt-caked sockets, his bloodshot eyes darted about fearfully when they weren't rolling from exhaustion.

He fell heavily on the ground where his men sat. They looked at each other with puzzled worry as their leader gasped and wheezed in raw, lung-bursting breaths. He could barely hold the waterskin Big Feather passed him. When he finally managed to bring the vessel to his cracked lips he drank like he'd never had water in his life, stopping only when his body's desperate need for air caused him to choke and sputter. Once he'd regained some of his composure, he still didn't speak; he just sat there, panting, his haunted eyes staring back the way he came, occasionally flicking nervously toward the lowering sun.

They sat like that a long time before Lame Dog ran out of patience. "Uh...Chief..." he began.

Heavy Collar snapped his head in the young man's direction and glared at him steadily, his eyes like blazing fires.

Lame Dog looked over to the other men for support. Big Feather began rummaging in his pack; Red Deer just raised his eyebrows and looked at Heavy Collar staring steadily at Lame Dog.

The lean youth swallowed hard and continued. "Where, uh...where's the woman?"

Heavy Collar's tense shoulders slumped a little, his jaw lost its clenched tightness, his wild eyes turned dazed. He looked around like he was noticing the men for the first time, but his eyes kept glancing back to where he'd come from.

"What are you...what are you talking about?" His voice was a croak. "I...I have no woman with me." He tried to put a grin on his gray face, but he looked like a death's head. "Hello, Red Deer. Big Feather."

"What am I talking about?" Lame Dog pressed. "What are *you* talking about? We all saw you running across the hills with a woman following behind you like you had her on a tether! Come on, Chief, why are you hiding her from us? Is she that pretty you think we'd try and take her?"

"No! No, no." Heavy Collar's rasping voice took on a pleading note. "There's no woman. There is no woman with me. Your eyes have played tricks on you. It's...it's getting dark." Again he looked off into the west. "It's getting dark."

"This is nonsense!" Lame Dog jumped up and started back the way Heavy Collar had come. "I'm going to find her and bring her back. Maybe she'll appreciate a man that doesn't leave her alone at night in the bottom of a ravine."

As he stalked off into the dusk, Heavy Collar called out to him. "No!" he shouted, hoarse. "Don't go! Morning! Wait until mor—" A fit of harsh coughing cut him off. By the time he caught his breath, Lame Dog was gone.

Big Feather handed another waterskin and a pouch of berries mixed with buffalo fat to Red Deer, who handed them to the chief. Heavy Collar tore into the food like a coyote into a calf. He was shaking all over.

After Heavy Collar had eaten for a while, Red Deer spoke for the first time. He'd decided to let the issue of the woman pass until later. "Chief, what happened out there? Why were you running so hard? You're half dead."

"Half dead. Heh, heh," the hungry man stuffed another handful of food into his mouth. "I was almost all the...all the way dead. There were...there was that war party we tracked, they...they caught me near where I left you. There were too many. Too many to fight. I, uh...I got away. I ran."

Big Feather spoke up. "You ran? For two days? A full war party chased you for two days this far?" The ugly hunter would never speak so rudely under normal circumstances, but Red Deer knew the business with the mysterious woman had disturbed him greatly. He was very proud of his sharp eyes; if he saw a woman, a woman was there.

Red Deer made a calming gesture toward his companion and turned back to Heavy Collar as the chief continued. "Yes...yes. I don't know...I don't know why they kept after me. I just...I had to run. I had to run."

"Well, you're here now," Red Deer said soothingly. Heavy Collar didn't want to talk about whatever had happened, and when a man doesn't want to talk about something he shouldn't be made to. Plus, Red Deer was sure there was some bad medicine at work here, and only a fool goes out of his way to make somebody else's trouble his own.

"You're safe now," Red Deer continued, taking the empty food wallet from his chief's trembling hands, "and it's good to see you. You should get some rest."

"Rest, yes." Heavy Collar's eyes were glazing over, already half-closed. "Build...build up that fire, will you? It's so cold..."

Lame Dog came stomping back into camp a short time later, swearing and cursing, and by then Heavy Collar was sleeping like he'd never wake up.

The next morning, under a cloud-veiled sun, Heavy Collar still slept and Lame Dog was still in a foul mood.

"Come on, Red Deer! You saw her, too. Let's go get her," Lame Dog's whined.

"Listen," said Red Deer in exasperation. "If Heavy Collar says he had no woman with him, then either there is no woman or he has his own good reason for denying it. Either way, you should leave well enough alone."

The younger man growled in frustration. "All right, you stay here and keep watch over him, and Big Feather and I will go find the woman. She's probably still hiding in that ravine."

Red Deer looked over at the misshapen tracker who was toying with his knife. "I saw her," Big Feather said earnestly. "I saw her as clear as I'm seeing you now. It doesn't make sense to leave a woman out there, whatever Heavy Collar says." Lame Dog nodded enthusiastically.

"All right, you two. Go, but be quick. We have to get moving. It looks like rain." The air smelled of thunder. Red Deer was anxious to be on the trail home.

He had no doubt there was a woman there; he saw the same thing they had. But the way Heavy Collar had been running, the fear in his eyes, the bald-faced lie about having no woman with him...Red Deer didn't know what was going on, but he was happy to pretend there was no woman if a man in Heavy Collar's state told him there was no woman. Unlike his companions, he didn't have youthful lust or delicate pride pushing him around. That cold tingle still coming and going across his shoulders told him all he needed to know.

Sighing, he looked around to see what he could do while he waited, and he noticed Heavy Collar's ruined moccasins. Red Deer knew how running like that can hurt a man, leave him next to useless for days, and someone in the chief's condition could never make any kind of speed with bare feet. He pulled the tattered leather shoes off Heavy Collar's unmoving feet and began patching them up. He wasn't much of a cobbler—he hadn't done a stitch of leatherwork since his bachelor days—but the repair would speed their way home later.

The work took longer to finish than expected, and by then the two other men hadn't returned. The sun's overcast disk was already a bit past its zenith. Red Deer looked down at Heavy Collar, who'd been moving in his sleep more frequently. He decided the sleeping man could look after himself for a short while and trotted up to the overlook.

He slowly scanned the rolling country before him. A wet curtain of rain approached in the distance, and a few dozen buffalo were lying down in the lee of a big hill closer by in another direction. But there were no people. Were the others still down out of view in that ravine? What could have taken them so long? A man could walk the length of that little valley five or six times in the time they'd been gone.

At last, his eye managed to latch on to a small flicker of movement, way off on the slope of the big hill Heavy Collar had first come over. All the way over there! *How desperate,* thought Red Deer, *can a man be to get a woman?* How far was Lame Dog going to track her? Red Deer heard a cough at his back and turned to see Heavy Collar stirring. Fuming, he ran back down the slope.

By the time Lame Dog and Big Feather got back it was late evening, a light rain was falling and Heavy Collar was awake. He wasn't much better company awake than sleeping; he was silent and withdrawn, and he flinched at noises from around them. Both he and Red Deer heard the two hunters coming; they didn't have the woman with them. Red Deer also noticed that they'd been running on the way back, and revised upwards his estimate of how far they'd tracked her before giving up. He turned his back and stared into the fire as they came up and took their places. Nobody spoke for a long time, until at last Red Deer addressed Lame Dog.

"Do you..." he began, but his lecture trailed off when he saw the look on the two men's faces. They weren't embarrassed; they were terrified, staring at Heavy Collar with wide eyes.

"What? What happened?" The cold tingle across Red Deer's back felt like a scurrying mouse under his shirt.

"We followed your trail, Chief," said Big Feather, not looking at Red Deer.

"Yeah?" Heavy Collar's voice was cool and even. "It probably wasn't very hard to follow."

"It wasn't. A blind man could have followed it. But the whole way back, as far as we went—and we went pretty far—there was only your trail. You were running alone the whole way. There was no woman following you."

"I told you," Heavy Collar said, looking into the fire. "You didn't see a woman following me."

"Please, Chief," Lame Dog blurted out, sounding younger than ever, "be honest with us! We all saw that woman out there, plain as anything. But there was no woman, no trail of a woman. There was nothing, not even a bent grass-stalk."

"And no war party either," Big Feather added. "What were you running from? What had you running like that?"

Heavy Collar looked at his companions one by one. Turning back to the fire, he pulled his blanket a little tighter around his shoulders. Rain fell in the grass all around. "You're right. I wish you hadn't pressed it, but now I think I should tell you what happened to me. Red Deer, please build the fire up higher.

"I'd managed to bring down an old bull that was on the bank of the river," he began, his voice flat and steady, "and I was cooking a bit of the meat down in a dry gully..."

The rain had let up by the time Heavy Collar finished his story. The usually pleasant after-rain air smelled foul, and the humidity sent a clammy chill down to the bone, as if it were nearly winter rather than late summer. No bird calls broke the silence as Heavy Collar stared into the fire and his companions stared at him, at each other, at the blackness outside the circle of their campfire. Red Deer had it built up very high.

After a while, Heavy Collar adjusted his blanket. "You should try to get some sleep, friends," he said, laying down and turning his back to the fire. "We'll be starting at dawn and traveling fast. I need to talk to my mother."

*   *   *

It was a wet and silent two days back to the camp. After that first night, when no evil dreams or weird horrors came out of the darkness to assail them, the men relaxed a bit. After the second night, they could even bring themselves to smile and joke a little—maybe the ghost woman's curse wasn't eternal. But they were still wary, glancing nervously at Heavy Collar when they thought he wasn't looking.

They'd decided not to tell anybody else until Heavy Collar got some good medicine and purified himself. Instead, they repeated Heavy Collar's story of being chased for two days by an enemy war party. Heavy Collar hated to lie, but it was better his people thought that an enemy was on their doorstep than knowing that he brought a death-curse into camp.

The haunted hunter sighed. The night's feasting was winding down and he'd gone off to the edge of camp to think, gazing off into the shadows. Certainly, the camp didn't seem cursed; behind him he could hear the familiar evening sounds of people talking and laughing, occasional shouts of victory or disappointment from men gathered to gamble. It was all so comforting, so normal. *Maybe,* he thought, *I should wait until morning to talk to my mother. Maybe I won't have to talk to her at all, if the ghost woman is really gone.*

A heavy rustle and snap in the bush caught his ear, and Heavy Collar froze, gooseflesh running up his arms. He heard a low growling, and the rustling became a loud crashing. The man's heart pounded in his chest, terror almost overwhelming him. He had no gun, no bow, no knife...he was alone and defenseless, and the ghost woman had returned to finish what she started. The growling grew louder and the thing in the bush came slowly closer. Heavy Collar wanted to scream, to start running again, but he was petrified.

Finally, the growling thing came crashing out of the bush. It was just a bear. Relief washed through Heavy Collar, turning his stiff limbs limp. He laughed at himself for being so jumpy; he should have recognized the sound of a bear moving through bush. She was a pretty big bear and seemed in a nasty temper, but she was nothing to panic about. *I've got to get my nerve back*, thought Heavy Collar, *or I won't be able to hunt even rabbits without soiling myself.*

He picked up a stone and hefted it. "Hey! This is no place for you, sister! Go home to your cubs! Go away!" With that, he whipped the rock at the growling beast 20 or so paces away.

The stone sailed through the air and knocked the bear squarely on her thick skull. For a moment Heavy Collar was pleased by the accuracy of his throw. But the bear didn't bolt, nor did she stop growling. Instead, she shook her head and turned to look at Heavy Collar. Her growl grew louder and took on the rhythm of a human chuckle. The chuckle became a laugh; the laugh became a voice.

"Well, well, well, Heavy Collar," said the bear in deep, rough tones that were obviously feminine. "First you kill me, and now you're throwing rocks at me. I told you there was no place you could hide from me. I don't care where you go. I will always find you."

Heavy Collar leaped up and ran at top speed back to camp screaming "Run! Run!" and waving his arms. He sprinted for his tipi. He could feel a big wind rising at his back as he ran, and the air was filled with a roar. "There is a ghost bear upon us! Run!" Everybody dropped what they were doing and scrambled to the lodges. Heavy Collar ran through the camp and dove through his own door, and soon his lodge was filled with people, including his mother. They all huddled together and listened to the ghost outside.

The wind was blowing hard and shaking the tipi. They could hear the snarls and growls of the spirit bear-woman and her heavy shuffling steps as she approached Heavy Collar's lodge. "These people are no better than dogs," she grumbled in a voice like thunder. "I will kill them all, Heavy Collar.

None of your people will escape." The ghost bear paced close around the lodge's perimeter. They could hear her fur rubbing on the tipi covering and could see the bulge where her body pushed against the hide.

"There is nowhere you can go, Heavy Collar," the ghost snarled. "I will smoke you all to death!" With that, the tipi began to shake as the angry spirit bear moved the lodge poles so that the wings of the smoke-hole pointed into the wind and the air came freely down into the lodge. The tipi began to fill with choking, stinging clouds of smoke. Children cried and people gasped and coughed, tears running down their faces from fear as much as from the smoke.

Through the suffocating clouds, Heavy Collar saw Lame Dog trying to cover his face with a corner of a blanket. "Lame Dog!" he called over the noise of the frightened people and the growls of the bear outside. "Climb up on my shoulders and fix the poles! We have to get this smoke clear."

Coughing, Lame Dog came over to Heavy Collar. Another man boosted him up so he was standing on his chief's shoulders. Others tried to brace the pair, but the blinding smoke and everybody's coughing made balancing difficult. As tall as he was, Lame Dog could barely reach the smoke-hole. Blinded by tears and smoke, ready to topple any second, he groped for the right poles. "I've almost got it," he rasped. "Just have to move this one over..."

At that moment, the ghost bear-woman roared and swatted the side of the lodge with one huge paw. The whole structure shook, and the precarious tower of people shook and toppled. Women and children screamed, and Lame Dog didn't move from where he fell.

"Mother!" cried Heavy Collar through the haze. "Do you have some medicine that will drive this ghost away? We have to try something, or we'll all die!"

His aged mother was the oldest person in the band, but she was still strong and hadn't passed out from the smoke like some of the younger people. Controlling her coughing, she fumbled in a pouch at her side. "I will...I will try." Out of her pouch she produced sacred paint and quickly made the right markings on her face and body, her shaking old hands moving automatically after decades of practice. Chanting as well as she could over the screams, the growls and the wind, she filled and lighted the pipe that had belonged to Heavy Collar's late father and thrust it out through a slit in the skin that covered the entrance to the lodge.

Her voice was thin with fear and the beginnings of suffocation: "Oh, ghost! Smoke this pipe. Take this smoke and go away!"

"No! No!" the ghost bear roared. "You people are dogs! You all must die!"

"Please, ghost," the old woman repeated, "smoke this pipe. Be at peace and go away."

"Foolish old woman! How can I smoke that pipe when you're in there and I'm out here? Am I a bird with a long bill that I can reach over? Bring it out to me."

Heavy Collar couldn't see his mother at the tipi entrance, but he felt the brief rush of fresh air as she lifted the covering and shuffled outside.

"No, no, no! Bring it closer. If you want me to smoke it, you'll have to bring it to me." The ghost bear's voice seemed to be coming from farther away.

There was a pause before the ghost bear roared once more. "No, I don't think I want to smoke that kind of pipe." The old woman started screaming, her voice tearing from smoke and fear: "Oh! Oh, my children! The bear is dragging me off! Help me! Heavy Collar!"

Heavy Collar rushed out of the tipi and into the clear air. The howling wind was whipping dust everywhere, but at least he could breathe again. With red eyes, he peered through the maelstrom and saw his mother being dragged along the ground by some invisible force. He shouted to the others to come help him, and ran to grab his mother.

His powerful hands locked around her birdlike ankles and he dug in his feet, but he found himself being dragged. His mother was being lifted up into the air. Heavy Collar felt somebody grab his own legs just as he was about to join her. Still, they were being pulled. Heavy Collar was above the earth at about a man's height, and the roar of the wind and the rage of the ghost surrounded him. He looked behind and saw a whole train of people grabbing on to each other. The whole line was being lifted. Higher and higher, and still Heavy Collar kept his grip on his mother.

When Heavy Collar and his mother were as high above the ground as the top of a big lodge, the old woman screamed and let go of her husband's sacred pipe. Instantly the wind and the roaring stopped, along with the force that was dragging them into the sky, and the line of people fell to the ground. Heavy Collar and his mother fell the farthest. Gasping for air, the wind knocked out of him, Heavy Collar crawled to where his mother lay. Either the fall or the experience itself had been too much for her; she was dead.

Stunned, Heavy Collar stood up and looked around, scanning the ground for his father's pipe. It was nowhere, and somehow he knew it would never be seen again—and neither would the ghost. His mother had used her greatest power and given her life to exorcise the tormented spirit of the murdered young woman. Saying a silent prayer that the girl might find a peaceful rest, Heavy Collar turned to the people who were still sitting where they fell, staring at him with frightened, red-rimmed eyes.

"Friends," Heavy Collar began, his voice hoarse from the smoke, "I have a story to tell you..."

The Legend of White Horse Plains

At the end of the 17th century, the political situation in what would one day be northern Minnesota and southern Manitoba was undergoing a great change. For generations, the Cree of the area had been slowly pushed north by the Assiniboine, who were in turn being pressured by their kinfolk, the Sioux, who were themselves being forced west and north by other peoples migrating away from European settlements in the East. Nudged over the years into poorer and poorer land, things looked bad for the Cree.

Things changed with the advent of the fur trade. As the people closest to the trading posts, the Cree almost overnight became many times more materially wealthy than their Southern rivals —and with their newfound access to guns and horses, they became a military force to be reckoned with. Such is the situation as our story begins...

The Assiniboine chief stood a long time watching the Cree party ride away north from his people's camp, until they passed into a fold of the land and disappeared from view. He wasn't alone in watching their departure; many of his people had watched the Cree leaving just as avidly as they had watched them arriving. It wasn't so long ago, near enough in time that wounds from those days troubled men not yet grown old, that the Cree had been enemies and rivals of the Assiniboine. Now, the chief had given his daughter in marriage to the dashing young Cree who rode away so proudly.

His decision would not be popular with some; he could already feel it. There had been another suitor, a Sioux chief, and it was with those people that the Assiniboine claimed kinship. But things had changed…things had been changing for a long time. Where once the Cree were said to be weak enemies easily raided, almost fugitives, they were now strong, with many guns and fine horses from their trading with the white men. Blood is blood, the chief told himself, but here on the banks of this river, between restless old Sioux to the south and newly powerful Cree to the north, one had to step very carefully.

The balance, though, had been tipped by the horse. Now and then he had seen its kind—snow-white, tireless, faster than the wind—but never did he imagine himself counting one among his own herd until the Cree chief had offered it as the price for his bride. Never had there been a finer horse; it was a spirited young stallion worth any 10 of his people's own mounts. And not only was it a prize in itself, it also showed the wealth and strength of the people with whom he was forming an alliance through his daughter's marriage. Even the most conservative of his folk would see, in that white horse, the wisdom of his decision…wouldn't they?

The matter of the Sioux suitor is trickier, the chief thought as he turned back to his lodge. He was proud and headstrong, that one, and had offered gifts that in any other circumstances, compared to any other gifts, would have been more than lavish enough to satisfy even the greediest of men. He wouldn't take his rejection well. He wouldn't take it well at all.

The chief put that concern out of his mind. He could deal with the Sioux later, after the wedding. After he had that horse!

*   *   *

The Assiniboine medicine man was furious. A chief's daughter marrying a Cree upstart? It was an insult, a betrayal of generations. Didn't he remember the Cree raiders, whooping with joy as they killed their people with those guns they had so many of? Didn't he remember the horses stolen, the women taken away? All that spilled blood—blood shared with their Sioux kin—washed away and forgotten in a moment of greed.

He sat in his lodge, staring at the low coals in his hearth, stewing. Yes, he had seen the horse. It was a magnificent creature, but no horse was worth trading away a birthright, and the chief was smiling while enemies were welcomed as new friends and old friends were sent away. Shameful!

Ah, but this affair wasn't over. There was still time to undo the travesty that covetous fool had brought among his people. The medicine man tried to calm his mind. Long years had he spent gathering wisdom and power in the service of his people. He knew the ways of the spirits, yes, but he also knew the ways and weaknesses of men. As long as he could walk and breathe, this insult would not stand.

Singing softly to himself, his mind filled with righteous anger, he began to compose his secret war song…

*   *   *

The day when the wedding ceremony was to take place was fast approaching, and the chief was becoming nervous. He had been told that, as he had expected, the Sioux chief whose suit had been rejected was red with rage. His people were nearby, camped less than two days' ride to the south, so the news traveled fast. According to those who knew of goings-on in the Sioux camp, it took the convincing of all the chieftain's friends to restrain him from riding to war immediately in retaliation. Instead, he was told, they had persuaded the young hothead to vent his anger in another direction, against more immediate and pressing enemies to the south. The Assiniboine chief and his relations had craftily selected that time for the marriage when the Sioux would be furthest away.

Now it was his own people that most troubled him. The whole camp was restless. Men he had known all his life were speaking to him in the shortest manner they could while remaining polite, and every day he would see groups of young hunters speaking with each other in low tones only to become quiet and occupied with their tasks when he approached. Trophies from the days of their wars with the Cree were displayed more prominently than ever, tales from that time were told more often. Snatches of war songs he hadn't heard in many winters came to him on the wind.

Rumor and gossip had free reign in the camp. He overheard his own daughter—the beautiful, strong girl whose hand was to be paid for with such riches—on the verge of weeping, asking one of his wives if it was true what she had heard about Cree men, about her husband. That he would… that they would…that when she was taken to her husband's people, she would…

It all set the chief's small hairs on end. He had very bad feelings, and for the first time in a life of action and daring he didn't know how he should best follow them. To call off the wedding would be a great dishonor—and he would have to give up that wondrous horse. He wished that he had time to go away, to pray, to seek guidance from the spirits, to recover the power of will he felt slipping away…but there was no time. He could only keep one eye on his restless people, and the other eye on the southern horizon.

∗   ∗   ∗

The storm broke on the day of the wedding.

The Cree groom and his friends and relations had just come down from the lake country to the riverside camp of the Assiniboine. He was resplendent in his rich chieftain's robes, and even the shabbiest-dressed among his entourage were dressed in finery an Assiniboine chief would envy. He was in no way making a secret of his wealth, which made some of those with a hard grudge against the Cree even more resentful, while others began to think that maybe an alliance with these people wasn't such a bad idea after all. Their clothes, though, were secondary to the horses they'd brought with them.

Their young chief was mounted upon a fine gray mare, a majestic horse that would have drawn stares and cries of admiration had its rider not also been leading the white horse that was to be the jewel of his bride-gifts. Beside that stallion, all other horses could only look like broken-down nags. Big, bigger than almost any horse any man had seen, it didn't seem at all bulky. Its powerful muscles were dense and sleek, its lines showing a perfection of grace and strength. Its head was high and proud, and in its gait one could see how it wanted to run; even walking, one could see its speed. All this, while shining brighter than the moon.

The Cree party was shown hospitality, some of it grudging and some of it earnest, but there was no comfort to be found in that camp. There was an air of nervous expectation among the Assiniboine that put the handful of Cree guests on edge; something was wrong here. But politeness prevented them from saying or doing anything that might give offense to their hosts. After all, their days of open war were long past, weren't they?

The marriage ceremony had not yet begun. Pipes had not been filled and exchanged, no songs had been sung and no dances danced before the first warning cry went up. In the south, a dust cloud was rising, riders approaching.

*   *   *

The beautiful young bride-to-be had just been led out of her tent, already nervous and afraid, when the shouting started. There was chaos in the camp, curses and accusations flying through the air, women screaming, dogs barking. Bewildered, she had begun to scream, when her father appeared before her, with his face flushed and eyes wide. Beside him was the Cree man she was to marry, atop a powerful-looking mare, leading a pale horse from out of a dream.

"Go!" her father shouted, his big hands circling her waist and hoisting her atop the white stallion; a large man, he could still barely reach the great animal's back. "We have been betrayed! Ride for your life!" With a slap on the stallion's rump, he propelled them into motion.

To the west, into the great plain, the not-yet-married couple rode on, the girl on the legendary white horse and the young chief on his gray, with the shouting of the camp fading at their backs. How they rode! They were twin moonbeams, one bright and one dim. But as fast as the Cree's mare was, the stallion was ever so much faster. An experienced rider, it was all the girl could do to keep her mount from leaving her husband-to-be behind as quickly as they'd left the Assiniboine camp.

"Go! Ride!" the Cree chief called. "I am lost, but that one can outrun the wind!"

As frightened as she was—of her Cree husband, of the pursuing Sioux, of the horse she rode—the girl was proud and proper, the daughter of a chief. "No!" she called back. "We are promised to each other, and I will not leave you!'

And so they rode, the tireless white horse straining for its speed as the gray lost its wind and began to flag. They jumped gullies, traveled through the low places, forded streams and crisscrossed their own trail to elude the war party that pursued them, but whenever they were forced into open country the bright white of the great horse gave them away, by day or by starlight. Finally, after hours of the chase, the exhausted fugitives slipped into range of the relentless Sioux's bows, and out of the wave of arrows that washed over them three found their mark: one for the young Cree chief, one for his gray mare, one for his loyal bride-to-be.

The white stallion, though, they couldn't kill. Freed from the weight of his rider, that giant among horses sped on as though he were fresh. For days, for weeks, the Sioux hunted that great animal, trying to snare him, corral him, lure him into a trap to be taken as a prize. But never did he allow himself to be caught. People began to regard him as supernatural, passing stories between one another of how the dying bride's spirit had joined that of her horse, how together they would run forever and never be captured. For years, people continued to catch glimpses of the uncatchable, unkillable horse on those plains—for many more years, in fact, than any horse could be expected to live. The white horse had become a ghost, a spirit being, running forever across the plains.

This all happened a very long time ago, over 400 years in the past, before white men settled in the area. But that part of the land, where the lake country ends and the edge of the great western prairie begins, is still to this day known as the White Horse Plains. And still the White Horse runs.

Blue Jay Goes to Ghost Town

The trickster figures of Native mythology interact often with ghosts and spirits. As beings operating outside the normal customs of their society, tricksters are able to deal with the very frightening worlds of death and the afterlife in a way mere mortals cannot—they prank the ghost world, and their laughter allows us to laugh at death.

Of course the joker rarely gets the last laugh, as you'll see in this story of Blue Jay, a trickster-hero of the Chinook people of the Pacific Northwest. Blue Jay and his sister, Io'i, are major figures in Chinookan mythology, with the levelheaded and long-suffering Io'i forever trying to moderate and manage the misadventures of the impulsive, thoughtless Blue Jay.

In this story, Blue Jay's devotion to his sister leads him to some very strange places, indeed…

You've heard of Blue Jay, right? It seems no matter where you go people have a story about him, usually a story of him getting into some kind of trouble and just barely getting out with the skin of his backside intact. He knows all the animals and birds and trees, and sometimes it seems like he's got the last laugh on every single one of them. He's an incorrigible prankster, and maybe not the brightest guy around, but he's brave as they come—a real hero—and adventure follows him everywhere.

Maybe his greatest adventure was the time he took a trip to the land of the dead. I suppose you might think that's no big deal; after all, that's where we're all headed, no matter which trails we walk, and getting there is all too easy. But as with everything else, it seems, Blue Jay didn't travel to the land of the dead in the usual way. At least, not at first...

It all started when one of the ghost people decided he wanted to take a living woman as his wife, which happens a lot more often than you might think. So, this ghost man, he goes looking far and wide to find the perfect bride—for a ghost to marry a living woman isn't an easy thing, and this fellow wanted to make sure he made the right choice the first time. After a long while of ghost-walking along the river he finally saw his girl.

Man, she was something else! Tall and strong—but not *too* tall, and not *too* strong—she had the kind of face you'd see once and then dream about for the rest of your life. She was quick and she was clever...and she was wise. You could feel it in her eyes, see those old currents running deep. After a moment of watching her, the ghost man knew she was the one.

So who was this girl, this radiant vision of womanhood? Ha! Well, that's where the trouble began, isn't it? Turns out the girl the ghost man had set his dead eyes on was none other than Blue Jay's own sister, Io'i.

Now, you know how close those two were. Io'i was a little bit older and a whole lot smarter than Blue Jay, and she'd never stopped being his big sister. She was like his adviser, his guardian and his conscience in one. Blue Jay couldn't do anything without first getting advice from his sister, and sometimes he even asked for it. Of course, that crazy hothead never listened. He'd always do exactly what he wanted to do, dismissing advice he didn't want to hear with the same line: "Ah, Io'i's always telling stories!"

But even if Blue Jay never listened to her he was devoted to her, and he probably would have had something to say about it when the ghost man showed up to ask for his sister's hand in marriage. As it happens, though, he was off away from his people—probably doing something Io'i warned him not to do—when her ghostly suitor arrived bearing his bride-gifts, sacks full of valuable dentalia shells and other treasures. By the time Blue Jay got home and found out what had happened, Io'i was long gone away to the ghost village to live with her husband and his people.

There was nothing Blue Jay could do about the marriage—it was all legitimate, everything done right—but still he missed his sister. I guess playing tricks and causing trouble, getting into crazy adventures, none of it seemed as fun without Io'i around to shake her head and scold him. So, after nearly a year had passed with him getting more and more lonely and bored, he came to a decision only a hero or a lunatic could make: he would journey to the village where his sister dwelled with the ghosts.

Trouble was, he didn't know the way to the land of the dead. Well, he knew the one sure way but wasn't too eager to go by that route. He asked around the people, all the wise men, and nobody could give him directions; whoever he asked would usually tell him that he was crazy, and chase him out of their house. What Blue Jay wanted to do was just unheard of.

Getting no help from the people, Blue Jay started asking his other friends. He went around asking all the trees if they knew how to get to the ghost town, and none of them could tell him. Most of the trees, they didn't even really understand what death was. Trees just don't think that way, I guess. Blue Jay then started asking all the birds if they knew the way. He figured that since they're always flying all over the world and seeing so much, surely one of them could point the way. But if the birds knew where that place was, they weren't telling. After weeks of this exhausting detective work—having conversations with trees takes a lot out of you—Blue Jay was no closer to his goal than when he started. Discouraged, he sat down on a riverbank to think.

"Hello, friend," said a deep voice to his right. "You look like you've snapped your net and lost a fish. What's the trouble?"

Blue Jay looked around, startled, but there was nobody around. "Who's there?" he called, his hand going to his knife. There were some nasty spirits in the woods, and he'd long ago learned to be wary of disembodied voices.

"Down here," the voice replied. Blue Jay looked down at the ground beside him and saw old stone wedge, the kind his people used for splitting cedar planks, lying there in the grass.

"A wedge?" wondered Blue Jay. "Huh. I didn't know wedges could speak men's language."

"Most don't care to," replied the wedge. Its voice was like rocks grinding together. "Me, I've been laying here a long time and you're the first company I've had in a while. So what's your story?"

Blue Jay told the weathered old tool about his sister and her marriage, about his quest to find the ghost village, and about how he hadn't been able to find anyone or anything that could show him the way.

"Ah!" the wedge exclaimed. "How fortunate for you, that you picked this spot to sit down. As it happens, I myself know the way to ghost town."

"Huh? Really?" Blue Jay was really surprised. "How is it that a wedge would know something like that?"

"Think about it," the wedge grated in its stony voice. "Lumberjacking's a dangerous business. You don't work at splitting logs for as long as I have—three generations, by the way—without seeing a lot of ghosts go on their way."

Blue Jay winced, thinking about it. The wedge was right. Blue Jay himself had seen what happens when careless loggers get clapped between the two halves of a split timber when they spring back together. Not a nice way to go, and it happened pretty often. "I hear you," he said. "So how do I get there?"

"Not so fast, friend," the wedge rumbled. "I'll take you there myself, but you'll have to pay for passage."

"Pay?" replied Blue Jay incredulously. "What does an old wedge need money for?"

"That's not the point!" snapped the testy wedge. "It's the principle. You have to pay for passage. That's how this sort of thing works."

Well, Blue Jay didn't like parting with anything if he didn't have to, but he figured he wasn't going to have an easy time finding another opportunity like this. Grumbling, he fished a few nice dentalia shells out of his pouch and placed them on the riverbank beside the wedge. "There. Will that do?"

"Ah, yes. Thank you kindly, friend," said the wedge, cheerful again. "That's exactly the way it oughta be. Now, if you'll just get up on top of me, here, we'll be on our way."

Blue Jay felt kind of silly crouching there on the wedge's flat side, but once they started their journey he forgot his self-consciousness. First, he felt like he was falling. Then, he felt like he was flying. Finally, he felt like he was swimming as the trees and rocks around him twisted and blurred. It was a really weird experience, even for a guy who has had plenty of weird experiences. When the swirling and twirling and shifting stopped, he was still sitting on a riverbank—but it was a different bank, on a different river. He had no idea where he was.

"This is where you get off, pal" the wedge grated. "Up that trail there, you'll find what you're after."

Blue Jay stood up, feeling kind of dizzy. "Thanks, friend," he said. "But where is this place, and how do I get back?"

The wedge didn't answer. Blue Jay looked down at his feet, and there was only grass and pebbles. That old wedge was nowhere to be seen. Shrugging, he turned and headed on up the only path he could see. The problem of getting home, he figured, would take care of itself later. Blue Jay was never big on advance planning.

After a short walk through the trees, Blue Jay arrived at the place where he guessed the ghost town was supposed to be. His first reaction was angry embarrassment. He thought the wedge had played a trick on him, taking him to a deserted settlement. The whistling of the wind, the creaking of trees and the muted murmur of the river were the sounds behind him—no dogs barked, no men shouted, no children laughed. There were quite a few big lodges that at one time must have been really impressive, room enough for dozens of families to live in comfort, but they were all now in seriously bad shape. Their cedar planks were moss-covered and bowed, their broad-pitched roofs were sagging and collapsed in spots. The place was a dump.

Blue Jay walked through the ruined settlement. Here and there he saw the remains of village life: big fish-drying racks that could've held hundreds of salmon reduced to not much more than brush-piles of twigs and small logs, moldering and mouse-ridden heaps of bark fiber that was once raw material for nice clothing. He peeked inside one of the lodges. Inside were scraps of ratty baskets, shredded clothes, broken weapons, cold and jumbled hearthstones—and skeletons. The floor of the lodge was littered with grinning skulls, bleached ribs, moss-covered bones of men, women and children. It was the same in every lodge he looked into: a whole village of dead people.

At last he came to the far edge of the village, where he saw something he hadn't noticed before: wisps of white smoke snaking out of the smoke hole of the farthest lodge, the biggest in the settlement. Somebody was alive in this graveyard of a town! Blue Jay's mind raced, considering who it could be that would live in such a place: a witch, a sorcerer, black spirits, ogres? Clutching his knife, our worried hero crept like a hunter, silently, to the doorway of the crumbling old lodge. From inside, he could hear snatches of song, a woman humming softly. With the tip of his knife, he gingerly pushed aside an edge of the ratty old hide that hung over the entrance and peered inside.

Well, Blue Jay's heart skipped a beat and he shouted with joy: there in the decaying old house, kneeling at the hearth and stirring a cook pot, was his own sister Io'i! Hearing her brother's shout, the girl looked up in surprise. Seeing him coming toward her with his arms wide, she dropped her spoon into the pot and her eyes went white with fear.

"Blue Jay!" she cried. "Oh, no...you've died!"

"What?" Blue Jay was kind of disappointed in his sister's reaction. "No, no...I'm not dead. I just got lonely for you and decided to pay a visit."

Io'i's eyes went even wider. "But...but how?" she stammered. "The village of ghosts is...I mean, how did you...?"

Blue Jay just waved his hand, cutting her off. "Yes, sister, it was a difficult journey, filled with great danger and hardship. But you know me, when I set my mind to something, nothing stops me!"

Io'i managed to reply without rolling her eyes at her brother's bragging; she was used to that kind of talk from him. "Well," she said, "you should not have come. This is no place for living men."

"I'll say it isn't!" Blue Jay exclaimed. "All these houses, all filled wall-to-wall with skeletons." He looked around the building they were in, seeing that this place, too, was filled with the dead. In fact, his sister was sitting right beside a big pile of bones topped with a grinning skull. "Ugh! How can you snuggle up so close to those bones?"

"You think this is a pile of bones?" Io'i asked. "Blue Jay, this is your brother-in law!"

"What? My bro...oh, I get it!" Blue Jay started laughing. "Ha, ha! Io'i is always telling stories! This time, she tells me that a skull is my brother-in-law. What's next?"

"Just watch," Io'i replied; "You'll see."

Now, it was getting pretty late in the day by this time, and the sun had started its dive into the sea. As darkness fell, Blue Jay began to hear slight sounds coming through the still air of the deserted village, noises of voices and tools, the rustling of clothes and the patter of feet. When he would look where there had just a moment ago been a pile of bones, now he saw a person. Soon, the village that had once been a graveyard was bustling with activity. It was an eerie kind of activity, though; something about the people, how they'd seem to slide away from his vision when he looked directly at them, was really disturbing to Blue Jay. Plus, the place still looked pretty ratty, and was still very quiet. These people did everything softly and in whispers.

Blue Jay turned to Io'i. "Sister..."

"Shh!" hissed the girl. "Keep your voice down."

"Uh...right." Blue Jay wasn't used to whispering. "Sister, where did all these people come from?"

Io'i gave a quiet little laugh. "You think these are people? Blue Jay, these are ghosts!"

Blue Jay's scalp tingled and his skin crawled, thinking how he was surrounded by so many ghosts. Still, he made up his mind to stay with his sister. She seemed pretty calm about her situation, anyway. Seeing that old familiar look of stubbornness setting in his face, Io'i sighed resignedly.

"Well, if you're going to stay here, you should at least make yourself useful. People are just about to go out to their weirs and fish." She pointed at a boy walking past with a dip-net. "Go with that boy, he's one of your brother-in-law's relations. Do as he does, but don't speak to him. Please, brother, keep quiet!"

"All right," Blue Jay replied. "Fishing sounds good to me. Better than hanging around this creepy place." With that, he picked up a dip-net and followed the boy down through the nighttime forest to the riverbank where the people were launching their canoes. Blue Jay wasn't too sure of how he felt about getting in that canoe—it looked moss-grown and leaky, not the kind of boat you'd trust your life to in broad daylight, let alone on strange waters at night. He saw, though, that the weird villagers who'd already cast off were floating without problems, so after a moment's hesitation he climbed into the bow while the youth launched them onto the dark river.

It was a cloudy night with only a sliver of a moon, and Blue Jay could barely see two arm-lengths in front of his face.

He could hear the other boats around him, though, and as the boy caught up to the main group of ghost fishermen, he heard them start up singing an old fishing song, very quietly. It was a little different than the songs he knew, but once he figured out how it went, Blue Jay joined in enthusiastically. But as soon as he started singing, everybody else stopped. He couldn't hear anything from the other boats.

Well, that hurt Blue Jay's pride a little; he'd always thought he had a pretty good singing voice. Annoyed, he let his fishing song trail off. He looked back to the stern of the canoe, to make a comment to his guide about the rudeness of these people, but where the boy had been was only a paddle and a skull resting on top of a jumbled pile of mouldy bones. Shocked, Blue Jay turned back around and tried to concentrate on paddling the canoe alone. Pretty soon, he heard the quiet singing of the other fishermen start up again and felt the force of the boy's resumed paddling.

He looked back to the stern and there was the ghost boy, looking none the worse for wear—though even when they looked human, there was something about these people that gave Blue Jay the willies. He decided to try a little experiment: "How far is it to your fish trap?" he whispered softly.

"It's just up the river, not very far," the youth muttered in a low voice.

A short time later, Blue Jay turned around and asked the boy again, this time in a hearty voice: "How much farther is it to your fish trap?" Right before his eyes, the ghost boy lost his human shape and tumbled into a jumbled skeleton. After a while he tried again, once more whispering, "Where is your fish trap?"

"Right here," the boy hissed, giving Blue Jay a look that made the little hairs on his arms stand up. Our hero figured it was best not to fool with the ghost boy any further, so he followed the others' lead and started fishing, sending his dip-net down again and again into the dark water of the dammed-up river.

Never before had Blue Jay had such terrible luck fishing! The first time he put his net down he felt it fill up with something heavy right away, but when he pulled it back up he had only two waterlogged branches instead of fat salmon. Grumbling, he tossed the wood back into the river and dipped his net again. This time when he pulled it up, the basket was filled to capacity with leaves and chips of bark. He threw this catch out, too, and dipped again, hauling up some more leaves and another branch. Swearing under his breath he tossed the rubbish back into the water, but some of the leaves fell back into the boat. Before he could fling them into the river, the boy gathered them up onto his fishing mat, giving Blue Jay another nasty glare. Blue Jay shrugged—if the dumb kid wanted to gather leaves, he was welcome to them—and tried his luck one more time.

When he brought up another two sticks, he decided he'd had it with fishing for the night. There's only so much frustration a guy can take before he calls it a day—or night, as the case may be. He saved those last two branches, thinking Io'i could use them to make a fire, and with a resigned sigh, he closed his eyes and settled back into the bow of the boat to wait for the others to finish up.

When at last the disastrous fishing trip was over and Blue Jay and the ghost fishermen returned to the camp, he was in a really bad mood. First his singing voice, then his fishing ability—two things Blue Jay was really proud of, and he'd been made to look foolish on both counts. It didn't make him feel any better when the ghost boy unrolled his mat and a large number of trout tumbled out in a silver shower. He could have sworn the kid hadn't caught a thing.

"Our canoe would have been filled with fish," the boy grumbled as he set about cleaning and roasting the catch, "if this guy hadn't thrown so much away."

Io'i looked over at her brother, who was sitting over by himself with a mean look on his face. "Why did you throw away your catch?" she asked, though she suspected what had happened.

"I sure didn't throw away fish," Blue Jay said, scowling. "All I threw away was a bunch of leaves and some old logs."

Io'i tried her best to be patient. She knew from a lifetime of experience that it sometimes took Blue Jay a long while to catch on to something new. "That is our food, brother," she said gently. "The leaves were trout, and the branches were salmon."

Blue Jay was actually pouting, now. "Well, I didn't come home empty-handed," he said. "I brought two big branches for you to use as firewood."

"Wait here," said Io'i, as she got up and went out of the house. The place was filling up with the good smells of roasting fish, but Blue Jay had no appetite. He just sat, scowling, feeling like he was being made a fool of as the ghostly people went about their silent business, fading in and out of his vision.

When Io'i came back into the house, she was cradling two big salmon in her arms.

"Where did you steal those salmon?" Blue Jay asked. He wasn't scolding her, he was honestly curious. As everybody knows, Blue Jay's never been above a little light-fingered activity if he figured he could get away with it.

"I didn't steal them," Io'i replied. "I got these out of your canoe. These are the fish you caught."

Blue Jay gave a snort. "Ah...Io'i is always telling stories," he muttered, and stomped off to bed.

The next morning was bright but hazy, the sun was a shining silver disk in the gray sky. That's pretty much what every day was like in the ghost village. When Blue Jay awoke, he found the place once again silent and deserted, with only he and his sister walking and breathing in the midst of all those dry bones. The novelty had worn off, and now instead of being creeped out, Blue Jay was just bored. With nothing to do while his sister puttered around doing household chores, he wandered back down to the riverbank where the canoes were beached.

If the canoes of his brother-in-law's people had looked dodgy the night before, they looked even worse in the daylight. At first, Blue Jay thought they were logs. The wood was pitted and crumbling, overgrown with moss. Brackish standing water had pooled up in the bottom of the boats, and the carvings on the prows were chipped and weatherworn into unrecognizable shapes. They really were terrible, and after he'd seen enough Blue Jay walked back up to his sister's derelict house shaking his head at the shabby conditions these ghost people lived in.

"Io'i," he said, coming into the lodge, "your husband's canoes are really terrible. What kind of man have you married?"

"Oh, be quiet," Io'i responded, not looking up from the bark-fiber shirt she was mending. "They're really going to get tired of you if you keep insulting them like that."

"But they're awful! They're full of holes! I can't believe that I went out on the river in these people's canoes."

Io'i tossed down her mending with an exasperated growl. "Are they people? Do you think they are people? Don't you understand yet, Blue Jay? These people are ghosts."

Blue Jay figured he'd just let it go, and spent the rest of the long, boring day lazing around and skipping rocks. At long last the sun set and the ghost people rose up from their bone piles and went about their ghost routines. They went out fishing again, and even though he figured he might be throwing his life away in those holey canoes Blue Jay went along with them. It was either that or cause trouble with his sister, who made it very clear he was expected to do his share.

Now that he knew the trick of making the ghosts lose their composure, though, Blue Jay decided to have some fun. He was still partnered up with the ghost youth from the first night, and on the way down to the river Blue Jay followed a little behind. Once they'd walked a little ways, Blue Jay called out, "Hey! Wait up!" and the kid clattered to the ground, a real mess. Blue Jay hustled past the boy's remains and went on ahead. Just when the phantom boy was managing to pull himself together, Blue Jay turned around and yelled, "Hey! Hurry up, slowpoke," and down he went again.

As you might have noticed, Blue Jay is pretty easily entertained. He pulled the same stunt on every ghost fisherman he encountered, shouting out a hearty hail across the water and laughing as the ghost collapsed into a jumble of ribs in its canoe. The ghost people were getting pretty annoyed, but since Blue Jay was a guest—and since they couldn't shout, anyway—they held their tongues.

Blue Jay was having so much fun, it's a wonder he did any fishing. But somehow what Io'i had told him the night before managed to sink in, because Blue Jay didn't throw away the branches and leaves he hauled in this time. When he came back to the house, with a trail of bone-piles and aggravated ghosts behind him, he was carrying two big armfuls of salmon and trout. Io'i didn't know whether to be happy about this or not; she could hear the ghosts grumbling in their quiet way and just knew her brother had been causing trouble.

From sunrise to sunset, the next day passed just as boring for Blue Jay as the last. When darkness fell, he was in the mood for some excitement. Well, that's just what he got; before the ghost fishing fleet got underway, the news came that a whale had beached itself at the mouth of the river. Now, a beaching was a big event in those days. It meant lots of easy meat and good fat, whale oil and whalebone, all just lying there for the people to carry away. As soon as the village got the word, there was a big rush down to the shore. Io'i gave her brother a big knife. "Hurry!" she cried, "Go and get us some whale meat!"

Blue Jay followed after the crowd of ghosts down to the sea, but instead of a big, fat whale hauled up on the beach, all he could see was the washed-up and waterlogged trunk of a massive fir. "Where is the whale," he demanded of the nearest ghost. The ghost couldn't answer right away, because he'd collapsed. Blue Jay hadn't even meant to do it; he was just really worked up about the prospect of getting a share of the whale. Irritated, he gave the ghost's skull a kick and stomped down to the beach where the ghost people were milling around the big log.

Everyone was already there, half-invisible ghosts busily stripping off the bark and chopping out chips of damp wood. Blue Jay didn't know what they were getting so excited about. Still, Blue Jay is the kind of guy who's determined to get his share even if he doesn't really want what's being divided. There was no place on the log that didn't have a ghost busy on it, though, so Blue Jay decided he'd make his own way: gathering a big lungful of air, he let loose his most powerful shout. All around the massive drift log dozens of bone-piles appeared, and Blue Jay scuffled his way carelessly through them to get at his prize.

Well, "prize" isn't really the word; he'd had his hopes up for hearty whale meat and delicious blubber, and all he was getting was some damp old fir. The bark was loaded with good pitch, though, which is always handy to have around, so he stripped off two big slabs of it and shouldered them to bring back to Io'i.

"Hey, Io'i," he called when he reached his brother-in-law's house and tossed the bark down outside the door. "False alarm! There was no whale, only a big fir washed up. But I managed to get some good pitchy bark, at least."

Io'i couldn't believe that even Blue Jay could be so clueless; she just stared at him. "Do you think it's bark," she asked, brushing past him out the doorway. "Look, it's whale meat, and its blubber is very thick."

Blue Jay looked down to where she was pointing and saw two big slabs of whale meat, loaded with rich fat, lying there on the ground. His jaw dropped, his eyes went wide and without another word he turned around and sprinted as fast as he could back down the path to the beach.

He hadn't been running long when he met a ghost coming up the trail with a big piece of bark over his shoulder. The ghosts had pulled themselves together and finished their work, and Blue Jay figured he was too late to grab more food off the whale-log. And as for the poor ghost who saw Blue Jay approach, he guessed what was coming and tried to protest in his quiet ghost voice. But it didn't work; Blue Jay let out a shout and the ghost tumbled to the ground, leaving that big piece of bark for Blue Jay to pick up off his ribcage. Our lazy hero stayed right there and pulled the same trick a few more times, until he'd piled up the bark equivalent of several good meals of whale meat. Laughing at the stupidity of ghosts, he hefted it all back home to Io'i. He was a bit irritated that she wasn't more impressed with his cleverness.

The next day, Blue Jay felt pretty good. Full of good food and pleased with his ability to lord it over the villagers of the ghost town, he was in a playful mood and came up with what he thought was a pretty funny idea. Going into one of the crumbling old houses, he picked a child's skull up out of the dust and cobwebs and swapped it with the skull of a big man. He took a man's upper body and mounted it on the hips and legs of a woman, and vice versa. He put one long leg on a short-legged man and gave a really big skeleton a baby's arms. He put some skeletons' feet on backward; others, he turned around their heads. Man, was he ever laughing! He couldn't wait to see the results of his handiwork come nightfall.

As you can imagine, the sun set to chaos in ghost town. The little kid with the old man's head couldn't walk or even sit up because his head was too heavy, and the old man with the baby head couldn't speak or see properly. The big man with little baby arms was so embarrassed that he hid his body under a robe so only his head peeked out, and the baby who got his arms just sat on the floor and cried, unable to lift the weight of two burly meat hooks. And the men and women who'd had their parts switch around? I don't have to tell you how mortified they were. Through it all, Blue Jay couldn't stop laughing; this was the funniest thing he'd ever seen!

But he stopped laughing pretty quickly when he turned around and saw Io'i, red-faced and scowling, standing over him with her ghost husband flickering beside her. He'd seen that look on her face only a few times before, when they were children, and he knew she was really mad. The ghost man mumbled something in the quiet way of his people, and Io'i passed it on to her brother.

"Blue Jay," she said, barely able to keep her voice down to a level that wouldn't turn her husband into a pile of bones, "my husband says you must leave this village. His people have tried to make you welcome, and all you've done is cause trouble and mistreat them. They don't like you, and they want you gone."

Blue Jay felt a little stung; nobody wants to be told they're not wanted, even if they've done everything to deserve it. Still, he didn't want to leave in the middle of the night, especially since he had no idea where the ghost town was or which way he had to go to return to his people. "I'm sorry, sister," he pleaded. "Just let me stay the night, and I'll leave in the morning." His brother-in-law agreed to that, and Blue Jay crept off to his bed while Io'i and her husband went about the night's work of undoing the damage Blue Jay had done.

When he woke up in the morning, Blue Jay was really worried. The ghost people wanted him out of their village, but he was totally lost. He imagined himself spending the rest of his days wandering the countryside, alone and without a people. He wished the old wedge would come back and give him another ride; he'd give that old chunk of stone anything it asked for if it would take him out of this place. This kind of uncertainty was rare for Blue Jay, and it made him feel even worse about his situation.

He was so preoccupied with his worries that he forgot everything he'd managed to get into his thick head about how things work in ghost town; that's the only way to explain why he did what he did next. Going to where his sister was in order to wake her and say goodbye, he saw her lying there next to a skeleton, her arms wrapped around its grinning old skull. This was too much for him to take.

"Ugh!" he shouted, grabbing the skull and hurling it across the room. "What do you want to cling to that disgusting thing, Io'i?"

Io'i sprang out of bed screaming and ran to where the skull had landed. Sobbing, she picked it up, cradled it in her arms, and carried it back to where the rest of the skeleton still lay. "Blue Jay!" she wailed as she tried to set the skull back where it belonged. "What have you done? You fool! Oh, you've broken his neck, you've broken my husband's neck!"

Blue Jay's heart sank into his stomach as he realized what he'd done. He tried to move to help or to comfort his sister, mumbling incoherent apologies, but she shoved him away. All he could do through the whole long day was sit there, leaning against the chipped and mildewed wall of the lodge, listening to his sister cry, watching her run her hands gently over her husband's battered head and neck.

When night fell and the ghost people once again had their phantom bodies, Io'i's husband couldn't get up. His eyes rolled and his mouth moved, but he couldn't speak. A shaman was called for, and when the medicine man arrived Blue Jay was hustled out of the house amid dark and nasty looks from all the ghost villagers. He could just barely make out the whispered singing and soft, soft drumbeats of the ghost shaman's medicine song as he sat there in the darkness, waiting to find out whether or not he was a murderer. *I wonder what happens when a ghost dies,* he thought despondently to himself.

Almost the entire night had passed before someone emerged from the lodge and came toward him. It was Io'i; her pretty face looked puffy and aged from crying and worrying. She was carrying five big bundles strung on a pole over her shoulder, but in the dark Blue Jay couldn't quite make out what they were. She stood before him, looking down. Blue Jay's blood ran cold, thinking nothing but the worst was coming.

"Your brother-in-law," she said in a hoarse whisper, "will recover. The healing medicine worked."

Blue Jay, relieved, stood up and opened his mouth to speak, but his sister raised her hand. "Shut up, brother," she said. "You've caused a lot of trouble coming here, and the people are very angry. Darkness or no darkness, it is time for you to go, now."

Again, Blue Jay made to speak and again his sister silenced him. "Listen, brother," she sighed. "Just listen, and try to remember what I tell you." She handed him the pole with the heavy bundles hanging from it. "Take these five buckets of water," she said, "and carry them with you. When you leave the village—it doesn't matter which way you go—you will come to the Burning Prairies. Save the water until you come to the fourth prairie, then start pouring it out over the flames."

Blue Jay hefted the pole over his right shoulder and looked at his beloved sister. There were dark circles under her eyes and lines on her face; he could see the track where tears had rolled. There was nothing more to say. He turned and went into the dark woods.

He was walking through those trees, up and down hills for a long time, before he came to the first prairie his sister had told him about. At first Blue Jay thought the sun was rising early, but when he broke through the cover of the forest he realized that he'd been seeing the light of the fires that burned in little patches all over the grassland. The wind blew hot gusts into his face.

"I'd better clear myself a path through this fire," he said to himself, and splashed water from one of the buckets ahead of him as he ran across the charred field. By the time he got to the trees on the other side, he'd used half the water in the bucket. He kept on going through the forest until he came to another grassland on fire.

This prairie was a bit wider than the last, but it looked like it was only burning on one end. When he got up to where the wall of flames began, he saw that this fire was burning really intensely, with big flames shooting up high.

"This must be what my sister told me about," he said. He didn't even bother to look for a way around or a route through the flames. He just dumped the rest of the bucket in front of him, clearing the path ahead. It wasn't enough to get him through the fire, though. He had to pour out another half-bucket of his sister's water before he got to the other side and headed up the wooded hillside in front of him.

When Blue Jay got to the top of that hill, he could see another prairie stretched before him. About half of this one was on fire, and burning quite strongly. As he still had three and a half buckets of water left, he felt pretty confident he could get through with no problem. He just charged right down that hill and into the flames, dumping another two half-buckets of water to create a narrow path; big sheets of fire rose on both sides, singeing his hair and clothes. When Blue Jay came out into the woods on the other side, he was fairly well roasted and covered in soot and ash. He was getting tired, but he pressed on.

The sun was high in the sky by the time he came to the fourth prairie, and this grassland was almost completely burning. It looked like a blazing sea, with flames instead of waves and smoke instead of fog. Blue Jay looked at his two-and-a-half buckets of water, then back at the big grassfire, and got a little worried. *Oh, well,* he thought, *nothing to do but press ahead.* And on he went into that burning sea, desperately splashing out his precious water to fight off the flames that reached for him on every side. When he got through to the tree line, coughing and exhausted, he had only one of Io'i's water buckets left.

He almost fell to the ground in despair when he came through that last forest and saw the prairie that spread before him. The others were like little campfires compared to the blaze that he was facing. The whole area was covered in flames; there weren't any gaps or spaces or burnt-out pathways he could use to get through. But he couldn't go back, and he couldn't stay where he was, so he hefted his last little bucket of water and ran to meet his destiny.

He eked that water out as sparingly as he could. The prairie fire was like a crowd of demons, with their burning hands all around him. His eyebrows were nearly singed right off, his face felt like it was baking hard, his lips were cracking and his mouth was dry as dust, but still he pressed on, splashing out water here and there to make his way. Through the flames and smoke, he could see the safety of the trees ahead when he tossed out his last drop of water. Taking off his bearskin robe he tried to beat his way through the flames, but the thick hide caught fire until it was burning in his hands. With nothing to stop the hungry flames his hair caught fire next, and soon his whole body was burning. And there on the Burning Prairies, Blue Jay died.

*   *   *

Being dead wasn't so bad, Blue Jay decided. After the nastiness of being burned, you got to have a nice, refreshing nap, and next thing you know you're laying in a nice, mossy hollow. There's a cool breeze blowing over you, the calls of nightbirds and the sweet rushing of a nearby river. Yeah, not too bad at all...

Blue Jay opened his eyes. Silver moonlight was filtering down through a canopy of cedars. How did he get away from that burning grassland? Where was he now? He pinched his arms and legs; they felt solid enough. But wasn't he dead? He certainly remembered dying, or at least, he couldn't imagine how he might have survived that terrible fire. He should be nothing but a ghost by now. And if he *was* a ghost, then that must mean...

He sat upright and looked around. *This place is sort of familiar,* he thought. He hauled himself to his feet and walked toward the river, hoping to get his bearings. Branches scratched at him, roots and fallen needles scratched at his feet. *Do ghosts get scratched?*, he wondered. He reached the riverbank and looked over the shimmering water. Over on the other side he could just make out the fires of a village through the trees and a few canoes drawn up on the stony beach. It all seemed somehow familiar.

Well, whoever those people were over there, surely they wouldn't turn away a lost and hungry stranger. Blue Jay took a deep breath and hollered across the water: "Helllooooo!" At least, he tried to holler, but something was wrong with his voice. Try as he might, he couldn't make a big noise. All that came out of his mouth was a thin whine, almost a whisper. He cleared his throat and tried again with similar results. Now Blue Jay was getting scared. Had he lost his voice sleeping outside like that? What was going on, here? A bit desperate, he kept trying to yell across the river.

In the silence of her husband's lodge, Io'i heard a faint wail coming through the night air. She dropped the dip-net she was mending and held her head in her hands for a moment, sighing deeply. She didn't cry; to be honest, she hadn't had much hope that her brother would follow her instructions across the plains of fire. Now he was dead, and in dying he'd done something no man before him had ever managed: arrived in the ghost town for a *second* time. Her husband looked over to her and nodded resignedly, and Io'i went out to fetch her brother from across the river.

Blue Jay's mood brightened when he saw somebody moving on the opposite riverbank, looking like they were making ready to launch a canoe. He hadn't thought anybody would've heard his weak little shouts. He sat down on a rock and waited for the canoe to come across. It was kind of dark, but even in the moonlight he could see that it was a good boat, a sleek craft with really nice lines. *Whoever these people are,* he thought, *they're doing pretty well for themselves.* When the canoe was halfway across the river, he heard his name being called out gently:

"Ah, Blue Jay! Blue Jay, my foolish brother, why can't you ever listen? Now, you're really dead!"

"Sister?" he called back in a hoarse whisper as the boat approached. "Ah, sister, it's good to hear you, even under the circumstances. Yeah, I guess I'm dead, all right. I don't think you gave me enough water to get across those fires."

Io'i's boat slid up onto the gravel. "You fool," she said as Blue Jay pushed the canoe back toward the other shore and hopped in behind her. "You would have lived if you'd just done what I told you. Now you have to stay here with us."

"Well," Blue Jay answered, sighing, "I guess there's nothing to be done about it now." He ran his hand along the wood of the canoe, admiring its workmanship. "Say," he said, "this is a really great canoe. I thought all your husband's boats were holey and moss-grown. How did he come by this sweetheart?"

"This is the same boat you went fishing in, Blue Jay," she answered, trying to be patient. "Because you're dead, now you see things differently."

"This, the same boat?" Blue Jay gave a whispery little laugh. "Ah, Io'i...always telling stories!"

They reached the village side of the river, and Blue Jay pulled the canoe high up onto the beach where the other boats were standing. They were all strong and sleek, solid and carved by a master. "Wow, all these canoes are really nice," he said. "Did somebody pay your husband tribute, or what?"

"I told you, Blue Jay," his sister replied, continuing up the path the ghost settlement, "these are the same boats. You're just seeing things differently."

"Always telling stories," Blue Jay muttered, following after his sister.

They came up the path to the village, where warm firelight was shining out of every doorway and many people were going about their business. Blue Jay was amazed by what he saw: this was a really rich village. All the lodges were soundly built with good, straight planks decorated with excellent carvings and bright paint. The people were just as well-favored: the women bright-eyed and beautiful, the men strong and noble, the children lively and well-fed. The only thing that seemed wrong about the town was the silence; even the kids playing their games barely made a sound.

"Sister," whispered Blue Jay as they walked through the midst of all this health and wealth, "What place is this? Do you have a new husband, or what? This village is much richer than that run-down place you were living in before."

"This," said Io'i, trying hard to keep from snapping at her brother, "is the same village. This is how it really looks. You see things differently now, because you're really dead."

"The same place?" Blue Jay wondered. "Ah, no way!"

"Oh hush," Io'i growled. "There's my husband's house up ahead. The people here are still unhappy with the way you behaved when you visited. You must be careful."

They came up to the big longhouse at the end of the village. It was fabulous, the prettiest lodge Blue Jay had ever seen. Inside, Io'i's husband waited for them. The young chief was nothing like the thin, not-quite-there ghost-man Blue Jay remembered; this guy was tall and strong, with intelligent eyes and a fine manner of speaking. He welcomed Blue Jay in—*a little coldly*, Blue Jay thought—and they sat down to talk on rich furs around the big, cheerful hearth fire.

"So, Blue Jay," the chief said in his quiet voice, "I didn't expect to see you here again so soon." He didn't look very happy.

"Uh, well…" Blue Jay began to say, "it seems I had a little trouble on the way home. It was much easier to arrive here than it was to leave."

"That does appear to be the way of the world, doesn't it?" Blue Jay saw a smile behind that stony face. "Anyway," the chief continued, "you're here now because you belong here, brother-in-law. You may stay in this house. But you must do your part…and no more pranks. Agreed?"

Blue Jay, who had nowhere else to go, agreed.

Eventually, he accepted that he was really dead, and a ghost, and that this was in fact the same town he'd visited before. It only took five or six days for him to get that all through his head, and it took a few days more before he got used to being in his sleeping-place by sunrise. More often than not, he'd forget the time and end up collapsing back into a pile of bones in the most inconvenient places. Other than that, life in ghost town was pretty miserable for our dead hero. Since he had a ghost voice now, he couldn't play his shouting pranks; he had to work just like everyone else, which didn't suit him at all. Plus, as Io'i had warned him, the other ghosts were sore about his earlier rudeness and shunned him whenever they could. Freshly dead, friendless save for his sister and unable to leave the ghost town, Blue Jay was bored.

If you know Blue Jay at all, you know what trouble he can be when he's bored. He just can't sit still, can't live a day-to-day life like most people—and maybe that's what makes him special. He always finds something to get his nose into. This time, given the intolerable tedium of night after night of fishing and the disturbing question of whether or not he was eating leaves and branches, which he couldn't get over, he focused his restless attention on the most exciting aspect of life in the ghost town: the village sorcerers.

Now, when he was alive, Blue Jay never bothered much with magic. He knew a few basic bits of medicine, but learning the real deep knowledge of the ways of the world and the workings of spirits just always seemed like too much hassle. He didn't have the attention span to learn everything a sorcerer needed to know. But now, he figured he had nothing but time, so why not learn the powers? How hard could it be? Plus, he reasoned, these were *ghost* medicine men, so they must have some really strong magic. Maybe he could even find a way to get back to the world of the living...

So, he started pestering the ghost sorcerers, asking for initiation into their secrets. And every time he would ask, the answer was always "No." Blue Jay was just too frivolous and unreliable—and maybe even a little too dumb—for the kind of work required. He sure did have tenacity, though. Whenever the sorcerers, in all their mystical regalia, would set off for their secret ritual places Blue Jay would be right there trying to wheedle his way along, until one or another of the magicians would threaten him with some curse terrible enough to keep him in the village.

Io'i saw what was happening and started to get worried. She knew the way Blue Jay's mind worked, and after a couple days of watching him pester the sorcerers, she took her brother aside.

"Brother," she said, "you're heading for trouble again. You must leave them alone! Their secrets are not for you, or me, or anyone else to know."

"Well, why not?" Blue Jay exclaimed. "Haven't I done great things? Don't I have knowledge of my own? Why should I spend eternity fishing when I could be learning the ghost magic?"

"Brother, please try to understand." Io'i's heart was sinking; she knew her headstrong brother wouldn't give it up. "The magicians have been patient with you 'til now, but their patience won't last much longer. If you keep this up, if you insist on seeking what's not yours to find, it will go badly with you. The sorcerers of the ghost world are powerful, and they are not kind."

"Ah, Io'i is always telling stories," the stubborn hero muttered as he stormed off toward the river.

Blue Jay was getting angry. "What, do they think I'm a child?" he growled to himself as he hauled in yet another netful of leaf-trout and log-salmon. "Why shouldn't I be allowed to learn some of those powers? What do they have against me trying to better myself? Even my sister's telling me to forget about it, to just sit here and fish forever. Well, I bet I'd make a great sorcerer!" His thoughts ran like that night after night, until he built up a fantasy of magical power like you wouldn't believe. There was no turning back for Blue Jay, then. He was determined to get his share of the ghost-wizards' magic.

The next time the sorcerers headed out to their unknown rituals in secret places, Blue Jay was ready. His face blackened with charcoal, he used all his skills as a hunter to follow them silently through the forest. Along twisting paths they went, deep into the heart of the trees. They never looked back. Blue Jay had to bite his tongue to keep from laughing. *All their secrecy and hocus-pocus,* he thought to himself with glee, *and all it takes is one brave man —me! —for their secrets to be revealed!*

At last they came upon the secret place, a clearing of packed earth surrounded by soaring cedars, a fire ring in the center, faint moonlight barely reaching through the canopy of branches. From the shelter of the undergrowth Blue Jay watched as a fire was kindled and the sorcerers' chanting began. All our hero's attention was focused on the wizards as they began their dance. He studied every motion they made, moved his hands along with theirs as they made their mystical gestures, whispered along with their songs. In this way the night passed, as Blue Jay lost himself in the ritual of the ghost sorcerers.

*   *   *

The sun rose and set again, beginning another day in ghost town. Io'i was in her husband's house mending nets when she heard a sound like the whimpering of a dog coming from the doorway. She looked up, and there was her brother, leaning against the wall. He was breathing heavily, staring all around with wild eyes.

"Brother!" she cried, "What's wrong?"

Blue Jay didn't answer her, at least not in any way she could understand. He just rolled his eyes and let out a babbling moan: "Aauuugh-gh-gh-bubaaa..."

Io'i sprang to her feet and ran to him, clutching his arms. "Brother, please," she said frantically, "speak to me! What happened?"

Her brother's swimming eyes managed to come into focus for a moment, fixing on her face. A look of joy and recognition came onto his face then, as if he were a baby seeing his mother. "Aa-ba-ba-ba!" he shouted with a giggle, breaking into an enormous grin. "A-ba-ba-ghuuu-ba!"

His sister watched helplessly as he began to prance gleefully around the lodge, tumbling, standing on his head, scampering on all fours, babbling happily in childish singsong.

Io'i sank to the ground in despair, watching her brother as he tried wearing a cook pot for a hat. She knew what had happened to her brother. In coming twice to the village of ghosts he'd done what no man before him had ever done. But he pushed too far, crossed one line too many. With his mind destroyed by the weird secrets he'd dared to steal, her brother, the great hero Blue Jay, was truly dead.

Chase of the Severed Head

*In the following Cheyenne story, we can see how many elements
of mythology are common to cultures around the world and
across time. The witch-wife's demon lover, for example, is no less
than the universal chaos monster found in most world mytholo-
gies. The gaining of power through consumption (accidental or
otherwise) of the flesh of a parent is a major theme in mytho-
logical magic, and the children's desperate journey is itself an
example of the "obstacle chase" type of story, a very common
myth format.*

*These elements of universal myth are made more striking when
the events of "Chase of the Severed Head" are read as symbolic of
the history of the Cheyenne people. Just as the children of the story
are forced from their woodland lives, so were the Cheyenne once
pushed westward from their original lands. Originally a settled
agricultural people, migratory pressures by the mid-1800s had
forced them to adapt to a nomadic plains lifestyle. In this light,
our heroine's final sacrifice of her digging tool—indispensable to
a farm girl—becomes powerfully symbolic.*

The sun had yet to rise above the hills surrounding the lake,
but the sky reflected in the shimmering water was already
bright gray. That sky was a roof; the sleeping hills were walls.
The whole misty valley was a great lodge with a shining,

liquid floor. It was a quiet lodge, too; the birds knew not to speak too loudly in that place.

The woman stood on the shore, wavelets kissing her feet, and looked at the water. Her deerhide water bucket lay forgotten on the pebbly beach behind her. She looked out across the lake and watched the brightening sky in its ripples. The reflections flashed and sparkled on the surface. It was just the mask the lake wore. The water wasn't bright and clear. It was black, and the blackness went down forever. She shivered and smiled.

She wore a pale buckskin dress embroidered with porcupine quills. Once beautiful, her dress was now stained and worn, carelessly mended where it had been mended at all. Only the quillwork was in good condition, but that wasn't her doing, it was her daughter's. She didn't care about her dress now. At one time she had cared, back when she lived with her people. But she'd been a willful girl who followed her own path and wouldn't be ruled by fools. Shunned and mocked, the best husband she could have arranged for her was a luckless, lazy hunter. She had always been after him for nicer things, more meat, more and better everything. But since her dreams had led them here, she no longer cared about more and better. She didn't care about dresses anymore.

She pulled her dress up over her head and dropped it on the beach behind her. The morning air was cold, but she didn't care. She was breathing heavily; her heart was pounding. Slowly she began to unbraid her hair, and it fell across her shoulders like dark water. As she moved, she saw the red paint on her shoulders, on her hands. It was on her face, too. She could feel it there, itching. It was sacred paint, medicine paint. Her husband had put it on her that morning, as he did every morning to protect her from evil spirits.

Inside her heart, she laughed scornfully. Her husband was lazy and stupid and weak, and his medicine was just as weak as he was. Its feeble power tingled on her skin, but it was nothing compared to the power of the one who was coming. Her husband's medicine couldn't hold her, couldn't bind her. To the one who was coming, red paint was nothing.

The sky was getting brighter. The sun was about to come over the hills. Gooseflesh ran up and down her arms, her back, her belly. Kneeling on the sand, she was trembling. It was time.

"I am here!" Her voice went out over the silvered surface of the bottomless black lake. No echo returned. She waited.

But she didn't have to wait long. The lake knew her. The water began to trouble itself; little swells and ripples appeared here and there. She was breathing fast. Now the lake in front of her was boiling slowly: there were sounds of bubbling, of rushing, all the sounds of water. The birds were very quiet, now. The lake was thick like cold blood. It began to rise up. First a little hill in the water, then a tall mound. And then he was there.

She made a small sound, a tiny wail of joy at the back of her throat. He was beautiful, rising out of the lake. Rising, twisting, curling and dropping back again, he was a living wave, a waterspout. The sky glinted off his ripples and waves, like a shining, shifting armor of light over an everchanging liquid form. Under that light was darkness, blackness, endless night. He was ancient. He was secrets and power. He was water.

The majesty in the lake settled down into itself, bubbling slowly. Close to shore, a shape emerged from the shallows. This was his hand, cold liquid crystal, writhing in anticipation toward her. His watery tentacle curved around to her side, as if to tease her. Breathing hard, her heart hammering in her chest, she gazed out at the lake. Her husband's pathetic paint burned on her skin; his medicine raged impotently against what was now coming to claim her. Each time she joined with her beautiful demon of the lake, she came closer to completion. Soon she would be one with the ancient black sorcerer, and all the secrets of heaven and earth, life and death would be hers to know and control.

The spirit's evil washed over her. He kissed her with wave-soft touches. Around her he flowed, coiling like a serpent, enveloping her like a burial robe. Feet, thighs, belly, breast, he touched, and with each touch came a delicious cold—a flow of water extinguishing the fire of the red-paint medicine. Ice water scoured her soul and she gave a strangled scream of joy as her world exploded into liquid fragments of light and darkness.

When she returned to her senses, drenched and shivering on the still, stony beach, the sun was past its peak and sinking. She felt the power raging cold in her soul, stronger than ever. *Soon*, she thought as she gathered up her ragged dress and her patched-up old water bucket, *very soon, the joining would be complete.* She and the spirit would be one, sharing forever the icy black power of the lake. She smiled an evil smile and headed up the path to her husband's camp. There was no sound in the forest save the sweet song of the lake at her back, echoed by the dark song in her heart.

*　　*　　*

Empty-handed, the hunter was returning home. Through the afternoon forest he trudged, not even bothering to move silently; he'd given up on finding game hours ago. The last meat he'd killed had been a single rabbit that had blundered across his path four days ago, and the rabbit had been old and scrawny, barely fit to eat. For a rabbit to reach that age meant there were few hawks or owls around—a bad sign. Since then, he and his wife and children had been living on what berries and roots they could gather, and even that sustenance was scarce.

How he hated this place! He stumbled carelessly over a fallen log and cursed to himself, and he was answered by a rumble from his belly. The lakeland forest should have been teeming with game; instead, four mouths were being fed on forage that wouldn't satisfy a deer. There was a darkness on this place, a bad spirit. He could feel it. The silence in the trees was unnatural, the shadows too deep and too cold. And his dreams, they were dark, too. Not evil dreams filled with terror, not the kind of dreams one could take warning and counsel from, just...dark. Deep and silent nights of nothingness.

It was dreams that had brought him to this cursed forest. Not his own, but his wife's. Whatever her many shortcomings—laziness, willfulness, indifference—she had always had powerful dreams, for good or for ill. Usually for ill. When she woke to say a harvest would be poor, a man would be killed in a raid or a child would be stillborn, so it happened. She never dreamed of good times for planting or good places to find game, and there was much whispering about her and her power. The couple was dirt-poor and shunned to the point of being outcast when she told him of new dreams she was having, dreams of a lake rich with fish in a forest filled with deer, its bushes creaking under the weight of plump berries. Heartened by these visions and with little left to lose, he took her and their two children, a daughter and a young boy just weaned, and they left their people to find this promised land.

He was bitterly regretting that decision, as he had almost every day since he had made it, when he emerged from the spindly, grasping trees into the clearing where their camp was set up. Bitterness flared into anger as he looked upon the place. Nearly half a moon they'd been here and still they were living in the rickety hut they'd thrown up when they'd arrived, a framework of branches covered with patchy old hides. Brush for their fire was piled carelessly. The whole camp was in a state of shameful neglect. Off to the side, his young son was playing at being a hunter, throwing sticks and dirt-clods at an old stump while his daughter, as always, had her head down over a piece of porcupine-quill embroidery. His wife sat in front of their pathetic lodge, braiding up her damp hair.

She turned on him with her animal eyes. "What have you brought us to eat today, husband? Nothing, as usual?"

Pinned by those eyes, his fiery answer turned to ice and died on his lips. "No," he grumbled, "I didn't take anything today. This is a bad place you've brought us to. We should leave before we starve." He wondered, not for the first time, why he couldn't stay properly angry with this woman.

"Don't blame me!" she shrieked. "If you weren't such a poor hunter, we wouldn't be starving. And it was your idea to follow the dreams of a woman and leave our people."

"You're right, you're right," he replied petulantly, like a scolded child. "I should have known. You can only dream death and sickness and bloodshed. I should have known that for you a dream of plenty means starvation."

"For you to tell all the things you should know, but don't," she sneered, "would take three days of talking."

Her insults didn't bother him as much as they once had. Why was that? He should be furious, scold her, beat her, do *something* a man would do, but it just didn't seem to matter. His heart was frostbitten. *Maybe she's right*, he thought, *maybe I am a foolish weakling.*

He tried to keep the argument going, to find his anger. "And where is your medicine paint that I put on you in the morning? Every day I return to find it gone from your body."

"Oh, your paint, your paint, your wonderful paint," the woman laughed mockingly. "Listen to the great medicine man talk. Your medicine couldn't stop a mosquito from biting me, let alone deter an evil spirit. If you must know, oh man of magic, it washes off when I bathe while I'm fetching water."

"Is that all you did today? Fetch a pail of water and take a bath? And you're only now braiding your hair!" The heat of anger was coming back into his heart. "Go, now! There's still plenty of daylight left. Go and gather us something to eat. Even a useless thing like you can be expected to do that much."

She locked her eyes on his, and he could see the hate and scorn in her face. He could feel the cold of her soul. More than anything, he wanted to look away, to have her leave him alone. The little ember of his rage was nearly extinguished when at last the woman looked away, slapping her hands on her thighs as she stood up.

"Hah! I suppose I must be the one to feed us, since you hunt about as well as your son tossing dirt over there. So be it. Daughter, put down that embroidery and come with me."

"No," said the man, "leave her here. She, at least, knows how to busy herself with the work of a woman."

Again their eyes locked, but his wife had lost her animal look. After a moment, she simply snorted derisively and stomped off into the bush. When he could no longer make out the crash and snap of her passage through the trees, he turned to his daughter. Though the hide she was working on was of poor quality, her beadwork was exceptional. If only her mother hadn't made them leave their people, if only her mother's reputation hadn't tainted her, she would have made some young man an excellent wife.

"Daughter," he said, "tell me what your mother does when I leave in the morning."

"Every day, after you put your medicine paint on her and go off to hunt," the girl replied, looking up from her beading, "she goes to fetch water, Father."

"I see. And then what?"

"And then nothing, Father. When she goes for water, she doesn't come back until just before you return. While she's gone," the girl added with timid pride, "I look after my brother."

"Good girl," her father muttered distractedly. He fell silent and stared into the gathering dusk while his dutiful girl returned to the colorful pattern of dyed porcupine quills in her hands.

The man's mind was clear; his hunger forgotten. His wife had a lover! Anger rose up inside him, filling his veins with heat. With no sound around but the whispering of the trees and the irregular thumping of his son's target practice, the man sat and made his plan for the morning.

*   *   *

The shore of the dark lake was cold in the early dawn, a cold unnatural for the season. Thick swirls of mist rose up off the waters, sending ghostly damp fingers deep into the world, sucking light and heat, swallowing sound and motion. There was no birdsong to keep him company as he shivered in his hiding place, clutching his good big knife. There was nothing but the gray air, still and chill as death.

He'd gone about his usual business that morning, eating a handful of shriveled sour berries before anointing his wife with his sacred paint. She'd sneered and laughed while he performed the ritual, but he swallowed his anger—he suspected now that she'd been witching him, using her unnatural power to cool his will. He wanted her to lead him to this place where she spent all her days.

When he'd finished her, he gathered his hunting gear and went off some distance into the woods before doubling back to the stark pebbles of the lakeshore. At the edge of the forest he'd scraped out a shallow hole and built a hasty hunting-blind of brush, concealing himself there, waiting for his unfaithful wife to make her tryst. He didn't know from what people her lover came, what blood he'd be spilling that he might have to answer for one day, and he didn't at that moment care. He had a burning song of vengeance in his heart.

A sound of footsteps on the stony path to the lake brought him back from his red thoughts. Peering from his blind, he watched his wife come into view carrying her skin bucket. This she let fall from her fingers as she strode down to the water's edge. Despite the chill, which seemed to be deepening despite the imminent sunrise, she pulled off her dress and tossed it onto the pebbles. As he watched, she began to unbraid her hair.

What shamelessness, he thought as his jealousy seethed, *she's so eager, she doesn't even wait for her lover to arrive before undressing herself.*

When his wife had loosened her hair to straggle over her shoulders, she did something he didn't understand. She knelt down on the rocky beach so that her knees were in the water. Gazing steadily across the shimmering surface of the black lake, she raised her arms as if in prayer and called out into the mist.

"I am here!" she cried. The damp air swallowed the echoes of her shout.

Immediately the hidden hunter knew something was very wrong, that his witch-wife wasn't simply summoning some man paddling across the lake. Gooseflesh rose on his arms as the air seemed to thicken and its temperature dropped even farther still. The feeling of evil that had always been about the place intensified many times; locking his limbs in fear, his knuckles turned white around the handle of his knife. His wife was staring across the water with wide eyes, her mouth open in a silent shout of pleasure, and he followed her gaze onto the lake.

The black water was boiling and rolling impossibly, rising up into grotesque mounds of undulating water before plunging to form black valleys. Again and again it rose and fell, the misty valley filling with a sound like the breathing of a drowning giant. The liquid darkness flashed with reflections of foul silver. The man had heard the stories of his people, and somewhere in his mind he knew he was seeing a *mih'ni*, a water spirit.

As the man watched, frozen, the chaos in the lake subsided into a slow roll with none of the rhythm of natural waves, and the noise died to a ragged, gurgling rumble. Nearer to the waterline, a more distinct form began to emerge from the cursed lake: a writhing tentacle of dark water waving to and fro searching out its prey. Inexorably it made its way to the pebble beach where his wife waited in rapture.

Nausea filled the cowering man as he watched the liquid limb of the *mih'ni* move to caress his witch-wife's thigh. He despaired as he saw how the evil spirit disregarded his protective medicine. The spirit slithered his way up the woman's body, stripping the sacred red paint. It was a sickness he was seeing, a terrible offense against the order of things—his wife was consorting with a demon!

The hunter's fearful nausea began to transform itself into rage at the union taking place before him. As the watery spirit moved itself up to the woman's face and began flowing into her mouth, the fear and disgust and anger caught fire in his soul. Mad with fury, he exploded into action.

Screaming a war-cry from the depths of madness he scattered the brush of his blind and charged across the beach, his big knife held high. In the time it takes to blink an eye he was upon the unholy couple, swinging that weapon with all his strength and then some. The knife passed through the tentacle of the *mih'ni* again and again as the man screamed, scattering it into shining droplets. The bubbling rumble over the lake rose once more into a sudden roar as the water spirit recoiled from the hunter's crazed attack. At last there was nothing left of that part of the demon save a few scattered pools of water, some of which still rippled limply, attempting to return to the lake.

As he set upon the water spirit, severing its watery limb that flowed over his wife's body, the demon-possessed woman fell to the pebbles in a swoon. She began to twitch and gag, coughing up some of the water that entered her body. Hearing her stir, the enraged man now turned his glistening knife on his unfaithful wife. With a final shout, he chopped through her neck with one stroke, grabbing her head by the

hair and flinging it far out into the black lake where still the
mih'ni bubbled, yelling, "Take your wife!"

The gurgling howl of the water spirit filled the valley,
but no new horrors rose from the lake. The churning of
the water's surface subsided, the roaring died away and the
unnatural chill began to dissipate until the man was alone on
the gray beach, gasping like a wounded animal.

He looked down at the body of his wife still pouring red
out onto the stones. The blood-madness had not left him; the
rage that gave him power to fight a demon had burned up
his mind. He thought of the witch, of the children she had
given him, and in his madness he knew his revenge was not
yet complete. Kneeling down beside the waterlogged corpse,
already as cold as if she had been dead a day, the hunter raised
his knife and went to work.

*   *   *

With her quillwork in her hands, the girl could almost forget her empty belly. The rhythm of the awl and the porcupine
quills lulled her as the bright pattern built up bit by bit on the
soft hide, the last piece of good tanned hide the family had.
The scarcity of game meant no skins as well as no meat, and
it pained her almost as much as her hunger.

As she worked, she kept an ear on her little brother playing
nearby. Only just weaned from their mother's breast, he was
already playing at being a hunter and a warrior, ferociously
attacking tree stumps and fallen logs with sticks and stones,
making brave little war-whoops. But poverty was gnawing at
his childish energy, and he didn't stalk his wooden prey and
shout down his mossy enemies with the same vigor. Berries
and roots aren't enough for a boy to grow on. He didn't fuss

over his hunger, though, and the sound of his make-believe warfare made the girl smile as she worked her brilliant quills into the leather.

She was just starting another row when she heard the sound of someone approaching through the forest and moved quickly to silence her brother, but once they heard the voice of their father calling out they jumped to their feet. If he was returning this soon, it could only mean he'd had luck hunting, and the thought of a sizzling piece of meat dripping with fat made the girl's mouth water. Sure enough, when her father marched out of the tree cover, his game bag was hanging heavy at his side.

"Children," he called out, smiling, "I brought some meat, a young deer! Come, I'll make something for you to eat."

From his bag he pulled the cut he'd brought, a small side of ribs from a deer that couldn't have been more than a fawn. Still, meat was meat, and the children watched hungrily as their father cut flesh and fat from the bones, then cracked the bones for marrow and began stewing it all over the fire. As the delicious smell began to fill the air, making even their ratty little lodge feel cozy, the girl remembered her other concern.

"Father," she asked, "what about the deer's hide? If it was as small as this, you could have brought the whole thing back and I could have tanned the skin."

A dangerous, frightening look passed across her father's face before he hastily turned back to the cooking meat. "I... well, I thought it best to bring back a smaller piece quickly so you two could eat something right away. I'm going to go out and bring it back after you eat. Where there's one deer, there are two, right? Maybe I'll get us a nice, fat buck!"

Something about her father's manner made the girl uneasy, but the smell of cooking meat soon made her forget every other thought in of her head. Before it was even properly cooked, her father was scooping morsels of still-bloody venison into wooden bowls and handing them to the children. The two tore into the food greedily, relishing the taste of good meat after having had none for so long, with grease and blood dripping down their chins. After a few mouthfuls, though, the young boy paused in his eating and looked up at his father.

"This tastes like Mother," he said with a puzzled expression on his face.

"Oh, hush up, you're being silly," his sister said, jabbing him with an elbow. "This is deer meat. Aren't you going to eat, Father?"

"Oh...no, no," he replied, sounding nervous. "You eat, eat all you want. I, ah...I was so hungry that I roasted a bit for myself right there on the spot!

"In fact, I'm going to go back out, now," he continued, as he began gathering up his things. As the girl watched him over the rim of her bowl, he packed up all his spare bowstrings, his spare knife, his heavy robe, everything he had.

"Father," she asked, "why are you packing so heavily?"

Again the dangerous look passed across her father's eyes, a flash of hot anger. "So many questions with you! Just like your mother," he snarled. "I may be gone for some time...I think I may have found a good game trail, and I want to get as much as I can."

The man hurried out of the tent with his gear, almost running across the little clearing and into the forest. "I'll bring back some good hides, too!" he shouted back as he marched into the green murk of the bush.

The girl listened to his hurried passage through the trees with an uneasy feeling, but when at last the crashing and snapping faded out of earshot she shrugged and turned back to the fire to take some of the meat and set it aside for her mother. The meal was warm inside her, filling her fingers with energy when she once again picked up her quillwork.

All afternoon she worked on the colorful pattern while her brother ran about shouting and laughing. That food had been marvellous! She felt like she was working the quills and awl faster and more accurately than she ever had before. She hummed an old working song as she punched holes and pushed quills. But as the afternoon turned into evening with no sign of her mother or father, her well-being began to fade. When evening turned into dusk, her brother stopped shouting and came to sit close beside her, huddled in his robe, drawing little pictures in the dirt with a stick. Night fell, and the two children retreated from the darkness into the small comfort of their lodge, where they sat hugging their knees without speaking, staring into the crackling cookfire.

Sister and brother waited and worried a long time in the threatening silence of the night. Then, just past midnight, they at last heard the sound of movement in the trees coming from the direction of the lake. From inside the hut, the girl called out into the night, "Mother? Mother, is that you?"

There was no answer from the forest, just the sound of someone crashing recklessly through the underbrush. That uneasy feeling returned, a prickling of the skin on her arms and a strange sensation of warmth flowing in her blood. Something wasn't right, she knew. The noise in the forest didn't have the swishing rhythm of a person striding through. It was a constant rustling, like something large and heavy being dragged or rolled through the dry carpet of deadfall.

Whatever it was it came slowly nearer until it sounded like it was on the edge of their clearing. The boy's eyes were wide with fright as the girl called out again, her voice cracking: "Mother? Mother, answer me!"

The sound in the bushes stopped, and the silence of the night flowed around them again. For a long time, there was no sound; even the crackle of twigs burning in the little fire-ring sounded muted and dull. The terror of that silence filled the girl's soul; beside her, her brother was shaking, his mouth open, screaming without sound. But when at last a voice came out of the night, it was even worse than the silence.

It was—cloying and thick—the bubbling sound of a drowned spirit, it was a sickening mockery of their mother's familiar voice: "Is that my children I hear? Are those my precious little greedy ones who have eaten up their poor mother?"

There was a dull rumbling sound from outside the tent, like a boulder being bowled along the dirt of the clearing. The girl could feel the vibrations in the ground as the thing outside gathered speed and made straight for their lodge. That horrible voice spoke again as it approached: "Your mother's coming, my babies! I am coming for you!"

The tent shook as the thing crashed into it, but the framework of branches held and the skin covering stayed intact. Again and again the thing struck the sides of the lodge, but without building up speed it could only batter itself against the hide walls, shouting vile curse and threats. The boy began to scream.

"Mother! Mother!"

"Yes, that's right, darling," the sickly howl replied, "it's your own dear mother. Now be good, and let me in so I can show you how much I love you." The thing outside bumped insistently against the door covering. "Open the door! Open the door!"

The frightened young girl had to hold her brother back from pulling aside the door covering. Over the boy's howling she could hear the monster outside rolling back toward the edge of the clearing. Clutching her brother tightly, smothering his screams with her hand, she whispered harshly in his ear, "Brother, we must run away. Stay with me and run when I say so."

With her free hand she gathered up her pouch of porcupine quills and her root-digger, and huddled with her brother beside the door to the lodge. The thing had reached the edge of the clearing and stopped, and she could hear its foul liquid chuckling as it readied itself for its charge. It started rolling again, rumbling toward the frail little hut, making straight for the door. The girl could feel its weight shaking the ground as it rolled and bounced. When it was almost upon them, the girl flung the door open, keeping her body out of the door-way.

The thing burst into the lodge, scattering the fire in a shower of embers, and struck the opposite wall. The children saw what it was: the head of their mother, twice as big as life, with a mouth full of bright white fangs, a wild, wet mane of hair scattering foul water and a neck oozing black blood. Somehow the girl made her body move, shoving her brother out the doorway and tumbling after him in one motion, securing the door from the other side and sprinting for the tree line, half-dragging the boy. The thing in the tent screamed in frustration behind them as they ran into the night.

It was hard going into those dark trees. Without a trail or path to guide them the two children blundered through the brush blindly; the roots and debris on the forest floor reached up to trip them, while brittle branches whipped their faces. Through instinct and luck they stayed clear of the forest's dangers as they ran. But they were headed up out of the valley, and as the ground sloped upward, the boy began to tire.

"Sister, I can't run anymore," he panted. "I'm about to fall over."

He was still wearing the heavy robe he had been huddling in while they had sat in their lodge. "Let me carry that robe for you," the girl said. It was a big skin, but his sister took it from him and slung it over her shoulder; somehow, the burden didn't seem as heavy as it should have. Without the weight of the hide, the boy managed to keep up the pace until they reached the lip of the valley, where they finally had to stop from sheer exhaustion.

The sky by this time was gray with the day's early light, and for the first time the girl looked back the way they had come. Her tired heart sank. There in the distance, down in the valley, she could see the hideous rolling head coming up fast through the trees in big bounces, higher than the treetops. The thing spun and tumbled as it sailed through the air, scattering foul blood and tainted water over the forest. Where the evil thing passed, nothing living was left in its wake.

"It's coming!" she shouted to her brother, hauling the breathless child up and pulling him into a staggering run. "We must keep going!"

She should have been falling-down tired like her brother, but somehow her heart and legs found the will to keep running; she could still feel that strange warm power moving through her blood. But her brother was just too young to keep up for much longer. Gasping for breath, sobbing in abject terror, blinded by tears and barely lifting his feet off the ground as his sister half-dragged him along, it was only a matter of time before he would trip and fall, or simply drop to the ground. The run was killing him.

And if the run didn't kill him, the monster would. They had left the forested valley for the open grasslands, and the thing was gaining ground fast. Though the brother and sister didn't dare look back, they could hear the head's constant shouting. "Naughty children!" it called out in that sick, wet parody of the once-familiar voice; "Why do you run from your mother now if I was good enough to eat? Wicked children! Stay still so Mother can kiss you!"

It was then the girl had her first vision. With her breath coming in frantic rasps, her muscles screaming for rest and her feet bleeding from the cruel wounds of stones and branches, her mind's eye filled with a memory of childhood. She was very young, playing too far away from the camp, trying to crawl her way through a stand of cactus and getting snagged and scratched. She remembered the cruel thorns, the cuts on her arms and face.

"When I...when I was a girl playing," she said aloud in gasps as she ran, "sometimes the...the prickly pears would be in patches so thick...so thick I couldn't get through them." She felt that strange energy rise up in her blood. Without conscious thought, her hand dipped into the embroidered bag at her side and pulled out a handful of yellow porcupine quills. She scattered them behind her, and when she glanced over her shoulder expecting to see the grotesque severed head about to descend upon her, she saw instead that a great bed of prickly pear cactus had sprung up, stretching across their path as far as she could see.

The monster's damp voice ceased its oily wheedling and began to curse loudly as it hit the cactus patch. It tried to roll or bounce over the spiky patch, but each time it tried it would only get more scratched and further bogged down in the densely packed cacti. The children kept running until they could no longer see the cactus patch, and the rolling head's voice had faded out of earshot. Only then did they slacken their pace a little, just enough to catch a bit of their breath back.

They had traveled a long way across the prairie and were almost feeling safe when, over the swishing sound of their passage through the endless grass, they again heard the head calling after them: "Children! Children, come back to Mother!" When the boy looked back and saw the thing rolling and tumbling over the plain toward them, he dropped to his knees in despair and exhaustion.

"Sister," he sobbed, "I can't keep running. I'm tired."

The girl grabbed him up again and was half-carrying him along when another vision came into her mind, this one of her as a little girl getting tangled in the knotted depths of the bullberry bushes. She remembered the dark tangles and the wicked thorns, and she felt that warm power flowing in her.

"I remember when I was a girl," she said aloud as she ran, "the bullberry bushes...the bullberry bushes were so thick and so thorny a fox couldn't get through them." As she spoke, she took a handful of white quills from the bag that bounced along on her thigh and threw them behind her. This time when she looked back, a dark field of bullberry bushes had sprung up across their path, as wide and as long as a big lake. Again the thing that had been their mother was caught in the thorny growth, and again the children ran into the setting sun until the miraculous bushes were far behind them and the creature's curses were drowned out by the wind.

It was evening again, with the sky glowing pink and orange and purple and the wind blowing cool, when the two fugitives came upon an abandoned camp and dropped exhausted to the ground. As they lay there catching their breath, the boy still sobbing around his gasps, the girl looked around at the place. There were cold fire-rings in the familiar pattern, and then she recognized the workmanship of the derelict meat-racks and skin-drying frames that lay broken in the dirt. This had been a camp of her people! A bright hope rose in her heart. A full camp of people on the move leaves a big trail. She and her brother had only to follow that trail, and...

Her hope was extinguished by a cold, wet wail out of the east. The monstrous severed head of their mother had over-come the barrier of the bullberry field and was coming across the grass to take her revenge on her children. The girl didn't know what had happened to bring this curse upon them, though she could make a gruesome guess; she only knew they must run. She picked her brother up out of the dust of the old camp and they fled on toward the fading light in the west with the howling demon leaving a trail of death behind them.

They could barely move faster than a walk, now, trip-ping and stumbling across the twilight prairie, and it wasn't long before their grotesque tormentor was upon them again, still keeping up a steady flow of horrible promises and direst curses in that wretched voice.

"My babies, wait!" it wheedled. "Let your poor old mother give you a kiss! Horrible children! Your mother only wants to repay the favor you paid her! Stop!"

"Sister, it's no use," the boy cried; "I can't...can't run. Can't run. Please, I must stop."

"No!" the girl cried. "We must...we must have courage." She reached into her pouch and pulled out her last hand-ful of porcupine quills, these ones dyed red. The tingle of power flowed through her again as she ran, and she again spoke aloud—"I remember the wild roses I loved as a child, with beautiful flowers hiding cruel thorns"—before tossing the quills back over her shoulder. Behind her, an impossible mass of rosebushes sprang up from the ground, countless flowers blooming bright under the moon. The severed head screamed in frustration, cursing as it tried to work its way over or through the thorns.

This time, the children could only run a short distance before they collapsed to the ground with the monster's swearing and shouting still clearly audible. Gasping for air, nearly retching with fatigue, they listened deliriously to the thing's demonic mother-voice promise them death, death, death. Soon, they heard the head give an evil shriek of triumph and knew it had cleared the rose-thicket and was after them again.

"Sister!" the boy wailed. "Please, I can't run anymore!"

The girl knew this was true. Her brother was at the edge of death, but despite her exhaustion she still felt that strange power in her. As the head rolled nearer, filling the night with its profanities and promises, she thought about what she might do. All her precious porcupine quills were gone. She only had her root-digger left, and it tingled in her hand.

"When I was a little girl playing," she said aloud, "I remember often coming upon ravines and gorges that I could not cross." With that, she crouched down to the ground, and with the point of the root-digger drew a long line in front of her and her brother.

The earth shook, and there was a terrible rumbling sound that drowned out even the howls of the severed head. The children had trouble keeping on their feet as the quake continued, and the line the girl had drawn grew and became a ditch. There was a great sound like the bones of the world breaking, and the ditch sank deeper, becoming a ravine as more dirt fell in. Still the gap expanded, until the line the girl had drawn became a great chasm stretching as far as they could see in each direction. The walls of the gorge went straight down, so far it made them dizzy to look, and at the bottom they could see water flowing. The girl lay her root-digger down at the lip of the canyon, and it expanded in size just as her furrow had; in the blink of an eye, it had become a long wooden bridge over the great abyss.

The children hurried across, and when they reached the opposite lip the girl pulled the root-digger up off the ground. It returned to its normal size, and the canyon was left uncrossable. They could hear the demonic head approaching.

"Sweet darlings!" it called. "I know you must be very tired. Your mother is coming, my wicked little greedy-guts, and then you can rest forever!"

The boy sobbed and turned to run, but the girl held him back. "No," she said, looking out across the great chasm, "No more running. Now we will stay here."

"Let's run! I can run!" cried the boy.

"No," the girl replied. "We won't run any further."

The severed head came into view on the opposite edge of the ravine. Dripping tainted water and poisonous blood, it rolled and bounced along the edge, looking for a way across, muttering curses and grinding its terrible teeth. As the girl watched, she saw the grass and plants on the other side wither and die as the monster's corruption touched them.

"Darling daughter!" the thing that had been her mother called out. "Where did you cross? How did you cross? Oh, make your bridge again so that your dear old mother can come see you!"

The girl lifted the tool, feeling the strength in it, and was about to set it down when her brother leaped up and pulled on her arm with all his weight. "Please, no! Don't do it!" he wailed.

"Be brave, brother" the girl said, shaking her arm free. "I must do this." But as she made to place the root-digger across the gorge, her brother again grabbed at her, screaming and begging her not to let the monster across.

Again the girl shook him off her arm, pushing him away with her other hand. Before the crying boy could grab her again, she laid the curved stick down at the lip of the canyon and, with a great creaking sound, it grew to enormous size and became once more a bridge. With a gurgling shout of glee the monstrous head of their mother began rolling along the length of wood, leaving a sick black trail behind it.

"Thank you, dear daughter," the monster gurgled as it rolled. "Now your mother is coming so we can be together again. Precious wicked girl, Mother's going to give you everything you deserve!"

The rolling head was in the center of the root-digger bridge; they could feel the chill of death that surrounded it, smell its evil corruption, hear the sound of its knife-like teeth gnashing in anticipation. The boy moaned in horror, crawling away through the grass in desperation. But the girl stood firm as the thing that was her mother approached. When it was almost upon them, she reached down and lifted the tool off the ground.

Though grown to huge size, the digging-stick was as light in her hands as it ever had been. With one swift motion she upended the stick, flipping it into the gorge. It shrank as it fell, and the rolling head fell with it, tumbling down into the chasm, screaming its bloody curses all the way down. It took a long, long time for the thing to hit bottom.

When her mother's shrieking profanities were suddenly silenced, the girl sank to the ground, impossibly weary. Behind her, her brother was sobbing in the grass behind her. They were free of the horror that had pursued them, but what now? They were alone in unfamiliar territory, motherless, fatherless, without provisions. If they were to survive to rejoin their people, they had a hard road ahead.

But first, the girl thought to herself, *I must rest*. Lying back under the starry prairie sky she let sleep take her, with the mysterious power still singing its strange song in her blood.

*   *   *

The portion of the story recounted here is just the beginning of the children's adventure. Just as the Cheyenne once had to adapt to a new way of living, so must the children, as symbols of the Cheyenne people, survive on the plains. With the aid of animal friends and the powers they discover in themselves, the children become masters of the wilderness and saviors of their people...

Part II:

Stories by Amos Gideon

Bad Son and the Spider Woman

The people who call themselves the Diné are better known to the world as the Navajo. The following story is based on the legend of Spider Woman, one of the Diné's old gods who is said to live at the top of Spider Rock, which can be found near Arizona's Monument Canyon.

There are two kinds of people in this world. Well, not really—there are really many, many different kinds of people in this world—but for the sake of our story it is best that we focus on two groups: those who are born as blank slates, whose personalities develop as they grow up, and those who have personalities that are immediately evident, even during their very first few moments of life.

The children of Strong Broad Back and his wife fell into the latter group, as their two extremely different personalities were obvious before they were even born. Their first child never caused his mother a single moment's discomfort as he grew in her belly and did not cry when he was born or anytime after that. He always smiled and never woke up during the night. The child was so peaceful and quiet that they named him Good Son, because it was clear—even as an infant—that he would never cause his parents any kind of trouble.

The same was not true for their second child, who punched and kicked his mother as he grew in her belly and caused her to be frequently ill. He screamed with what could only be called rage the day he was born and came out so furiously that he almost killed his own mother in the process. From that moment on he never stopped crying, even when it appeared that he was asleep. Though he lacked sharp fingernails or teeth, he always seemed to be trying to scratch and bite anyone who picked him up. It was clear—even then—that, unlike his brother, he was going to bring nothing but harm and worry to his parents, and it was for that reason that they named him Bad Son.

Because they were so different, everyone expected the two brothers to hate each other as they grew up, but that was not the case. Though he was wicked, Bad Son was still capable of familial love, and he loved his older brother, who loved him in return even though he did not approve of his bad behavior. This was also true for their parents. Though they had every cause to love their older child much more than their youngest, they never said or did anything to suggest that such a preference really existed.

The same was not true when it came to their only living grandmother, Sees With Fair Eyes, who was not afraid to let everyone know that she loved Good Son but could not stand his younger brother. It was she who told them the story of the Spider Woman, while they were still very young.

"Though it may surprise you to hear it," she told them, "this world was once filled with many monsters, each more horrible and dangerous than the last. Some were even wickeder than you, Bad Son, though it is very hard to believe. These monsters made a sport out of hunting us when we, the Diné, first crossed into this fourth world from the third. But not all of the monsters were evil like you, Bad Son. Some of them liked the Diné and decided to help us so that we would survive and prosper. One of these helpful monsters was Spider Woman. It was she who gave Monster Slayer and Child Born Of Water the power they needed to visit their father, the Sun God, who taught them how to kill the monsters. Because of her help, not only did Monster Slayer and Child Born Of Water spare Spider Woman's life, they made her one of our most important gods. She was so moved by this honor that she shared with the Diné her ability to weave and gave them a loom made out of the stars, the earth, the moon, the waters and the sky that had been constructed for her by her husband, Spider Man. In order to watch over the Diné, she decided to make her home on the top of Spider Rock, which was high enough for her to see everything that happened in this world. She was a patient soul and seldom interfered in our lives, but there was one thing that would enrage her and every time she saw it, she would spin a web down to the earth below."

"What was that, Grandmother?" asked Good Son.

Their grandmother looked down at his brother before she answered him. "Misbehaving children," she told them. "Spider Woman could forgive all sorts of bad behavior, but she could not stand to see the sight of children who continually disobeyed their parents. When she did see such a child, she would wait until the night came and then come down to earth and steal them away from their parents. She would then take them back to the top of Spider Rock, where she would eat them."

"Eat them?" asked Good Son, who was clearly terrified by the idea. His brother, on the other hand, only looked bored. He didn't have much patience for these stories.

"That is why the top of Spider Rock is white," she informed them. "It is covered with the ground dust of the bones of bad children. Mark my words, Bad Son, it will only be a matter of time before you are visited by Spider Woman and see the top of Spider Rock for yourself."

Bad Son yawned. He wasn't afraid of made-up monsters that were obviously created just to scare silly children. If the story was meant to frighten him into acting more like his big brother, then it definitely didn't work.

*   *   *

While Bad Son may not have cared about his grandmother's story, his brother did. Ever since she told it to them, Good Son grew more and more terrified of the day his brother's antics would catch the attention of Spider Woman and make her angry enough to carry him away and eat him at the top of the rock she called home. He tried his best to stop his brother from misbehaving, but as tasks went, it was only slightly easier than trying to stop a stream from flowing by staring at it crossly. Bad Son could no more stop being bad than a snake could stop slithering or an eagle could stop flying—it was as natural to him as sleeping, eating and breathing.

Having accepted this, Good Son realized that it would only be a matter of time before Spider Woman came for his brother, so he devised a plan for what he would do when that day came.

*   *   *

Strong Broad Back decided that his two boys were now old enough to join him hunting, though he worried what might happen if he put a bow in Bad Son's hands. It was for this reason that he told his younger son that until he felt it was safe enough to trust him, he would not allow him to use a weapon. Bad Son was very angry to hear this and thought it was extremely unfair that his brother was not also barred from picking up a bow and arrow.

"Good Son has proven himself trustworthy enough to use a bow responsibly," his father insisted, "but I am afraid that you just might put an arrow somewhere in my back," he admitted honestly.

Bad Son couldn't believe it. Yes, it was true he was ill-behaved, but he wasn't evil enough to even think about killing his own father. Still, Strong Broad Back refused to change his mind and Bad Son's only other option would be to stay at home with his mother and help her with her weaving.

As he followed his father and his brother along the hunting trail, Bad Son sulked with a sullen scowl on his face.

"Cheer up, Bad Son," his brother said kindly, "you'll get your chance soon enough."

Bad Son stayed quiet. He decided to protest the injustice of this hunt by not speaking until they returned home. This actually suited his father and brother just fine, since it meant not having to listen to him whine, which—when he wasn't being petulant—was generally how Bad Son behaved.

They were out for almost the entire morning before they finally caught sight of a deer within their striking distance. Silently, their father nodded over to Good Son, who nervously lifted up his bow and aimed an arrow at the animal. He pulled the arrow back and then let it go. It flew through the air and met its target. The animal jumped up with surprise as the arrow pierced its back, but before it could run and get away, Strong Broad Back shot another arrow at it. This arrow was aimed much better than his son's and brought the creature down to the ground, where it quickly died.

Bad Son frowned as his father and brother celebrated their kill, jealous that he was not allowed to be a part of it. He stayed where he was, while they left to retrieve their fallen prey. As he stood there, he noticed that his brother had left his bow and his arrows on the ground.

It was a temptation that was too strong for Bad Son to resist. He picked up the bow and enjoyed the way it felt in his hands. It made him feel strong and manly. He wished there was another deer around so he could prove to his father that he was every bit as good a hunter as his brother. He grabbed an arrow from the ground and felt how much strength it took to pull it back.

"Bad Son!" his father shouted. "What are you doing?"

His father's voice startled Bad Son, and he let go of the arrow unwarily into the air. To the horror of the two brothers, it hit their father's right arm. Strong Broad Back screamed as the sharp arrowhead pierced into his flesh. Bad Son dropped the bow to the ground: there was no way he could possibly deny that he just proved his father to have been right all along.

The two boys ran to their father, who was in great pain, but appeared not to be as seriously injured as he could have been. Good Son told his father to lie down on the ground and ordered his brother to go and get some help, but as Bad Son started to leave Good Son changed his mind. "This is too important to leave to you," he told his brother. "You will probably get distracted along the way and forget to send anyone back. You stay here and I'll go."

His brother's words stung Bad Son worse than if he had been the one to get hit by the arrow, but he could not protest, because in his heart he knew that Good Son was probably right. He did as he was told and waited with his father. "I'm sorry, Father," Bad Son said with tears in his eyes. "I did not mean to hit you with the arrow."

"I know you didn't, Bad Son," his father told him. "We all know that you cannot help acting the way that you do—it is who you are and we cannot blame you for it any more than we can blame a scorpion for biting us. I should have known not to take you hunting. I thought that forbidding you from carrying a bow would have been enough, but I was wrong."

This did little to ease Bad Son's guilt. If anything, it made it worse because it was clear that he was a burden to his family and would forever be a barrier to their happiness. He vowed at that moment that he would be more like his brother, but he had made many vows during the course of his short life and he had yet to be able to keep any of them for more than a few days.

* * *

As Good Son ran back across the hunting trail for help, his first thought was not of his father, who he was sure was going to be fine, but of what he was now certain was going to happen to his brother. There was no way Spider Woman had not seen what happened today, and he knew that she would be coming tonight to take Bad Son back to her lair on top of Spider Rock, where she would eat him as punishment for his wickedness.

His mind raced as he wondered if he had the courage needed to carry out the plan he devised for this day back when his grandmother first told him of his brother's inevitable fate. Unfortunately there was only one way to find out for sure.

* * *

Their father's wound would heal. Strong Broad Back would live to see another day. As he rested in their hogan, his youngest son stayed outside and stared up at the stars, unable to forgive himself for what he did and who he was. Bad Son's stomach churned as he thought about all of the troubles he had brought upon his family, with this latest one being by far the worst. As he studied the lights in the sky, he decided that he could not bear to ever see them hurt, just because they were foolish enough to love someone as naturally wicked as he was. For their happiness and safety, it was time for him to leave them and live life on his own.

He stopped looking at the stars and stood up from where he was sitting and began to run. Where he would go, he did not know.

*   *   *

Good Son did not know where his brother had gone to, but this wasn't the first time Bad Son had disappeared without explanation and it would doubtlessly not be the last. It didn't matter though—if anything it was for the better—because it made his plan for tonight that much easier to fulfill.

He could not sleep. Time passed very slowly, and for a time he thought his grandmother had made up the story of the Spider Woman, but then he heard the sound of eight legs scuttling toward the family's hogan.

His heart raced as he jumped up to his feet and ran outside to face the god who had once helped to save his people. It raced even faster when he saw her standing before him. She was bigger than he ever could have imagined and—though it was very odd to use such a word to describe a spider—much more beautiful than he could have ever dreamed.

"I have come for the one they call Bad Son," she told him, as droplets of rain began to fall out of the sky.

"I know, Spider Woman."

"Where is he?"

"Don't you recognize me? I'm standing right in front of you."

"You are not Bad Son," she retorted.

"This is news to me. I would think I would know who I was."

Such was the confidence in his voice and the look of determination in his eyes, Spider Woman appeared to doubt herself. "If you are Bad Son, why are you not frightened of me? Do you not know why I am here and what I plan to do to you?"

"I know," he answered, "but why should I be frightened of an old woman like you? You are far too frail and feeble to scare a strong boy like me."

"I can see now that you must be Bad Son," said Spider Woman, "and how it was that you were given such a dishonorable name. Only the most wicked sort of child would say such a thing to a god.

With that said, Spider Woman spat out one of her threads, which hit Good Son directly in the chest, knocking him off his feet. She started back toward her home on the rock, dragging her quarry along behind her.

*   *   *

It began to rain and grew strangely cold. Given his selfish nature, Bad Son could only think of how cold and wet he was, and how he had no place to use as shelter.

This was not the right day to run away from his family and, assuming that tomorrow would be much more suitable, he decided to turn around and return to his home, where he would be able to keep out of the rain and stay warm.

By the time he returned home he was completely drenched. He had already started taking off his clothes as he walked inside, but he stopped when he saw that his brother was not there.

"Good Son," he whispered, not wanting to wake his sleeping parents. There was no answer. He ran back outside and saw something on the ground that made his blood turn cold—the tracks of a giant creature, if one were capable of believing such a thing. Bad Son saw a white, filmy material floating in a puddle at his feet. He bent over and grabbed it. It was a piece of spiderweb.

Bad Son felt sick when he realized that the story his grandmother told him had been true all along, and that Spider Woman had obviously mistaken his innocent brother for himself. He realized that she was taking Good Son to Spider Rock, where she would make a feast out of him and decorate her home with the dust of his bones. Quickly, Bad Son threw the piece of webbing to the ground and starting running, following the trail that ran along the wet ground.

He was going to save his brother.

*   *   *

It was a painful journey for Good Son as Spider Woman made her way to Spider Rock. His clothes and his skin were torn as she dragged him across the muddy ground. Still this pain was nothing compared to the agony that was in store for him.

To most people his decision to take his brother's place as Spider Woman's victim was unfathomable, but to him it made perfect sense. The proof of one's love was not in what you had to give, but what you were willing to have taken away. He loved his brother enough to sacrifice his own life so that Bad Son could live. If that didn't make sense to some people, then that said more about them than it did about him.

They had nearly reached Spider Rock when Spider Woman stopped and turned toward him. "Are you sure you're Bad Son?" she asked.

"Yes," he answered without hesitation.

She seemed to accept this and continued on her way.

*   *   *

Bad Son was running as fast as he could, but he feared he would never catch up to Spider Woman, who had four times as many legs as he did and could, therefore, travel four times as fast. As he ran he thought about his brother's sacrifice and wondered if he would have done the same if the situation were reversed; it occurred to him that he would soon find out, if he reached the top of Spider Rock in time.

*   *   *

As painful as the journey to Spider Rock had been, it was nothing compared to the misery that Good Son endured as Spider Woman climbed up the tall spire of stone. Dangling helplessly from the webbing attached to his chest, Good Son continually swung into the rock along the way up. They were only halfway up, and he had already broken an arm and both of his legs. At this point he was in so much pain that he was beginning to look forward to being eaten.

With still a long climb ahead of them, Spider Woman stopped once again and asked him, "Are you sure you are Bad Son?"

Good Son was in so much agony that he could barely speak, but he still managed to whisper out a strong and definitive "Yes."

Again she accepted his answer and started climbing up to the top of the rock.

*   *   *

Bad Son could now see Spider Rock in front of him. A bolt of lightning flashed behind it, and in that split-second of illumination he could see the figure of a giant spider climbing up to its peak.

"I'm coming, Good Son!" he said as loudly as he could. He prayed that his brother could hear his words and not give in to the despair that would welcome death to release him from his incomprehensible misery.

As he continued running, he was startled to notice that, though he had traveled a great distance, he was not yet tired and he appeared to be gaining speed with every step. It was as if he was being possessed by a much greater force—one that wanted him to reach the rock and save his brother as much as he did.

He prayed that wherever this power was coming from, it had not come too late.

*   *   *

When Spider Woman finally reached the top of Spider Rock, Good Son, bloody and broken, waited for the large god to sink her fangs into his flesh, but she seemed to be in no hurry.

"Tell me," she said, "what have you done for me to bring you here?"

"Don't you know?" he said weakly, with each word causing him agony.

"Of course I do, but I want you to confess to your crimes before I devour you—I want to know that you understand why you are being punished in so harsh a way."

"I disobeyed my father," he whispered to her, "and I accidentally shot him in the arm with an arrow. My carelessness could have easily killed him."

"That is true," she said, "but is that the only cause I had to come for you, Bad Son?"

"No," he said, "I also…" Good Son then went on to describe many of the other bad things his brother had done in the past, although he couldn't help but think how minor they all seemed to him now. He realized that Bad Son was often causing mischief, but the actual damage done was, in retrospect, minimal. If anything, his pranks and accidents had made life more interesting than it would have been without them.

"Yes," said Spider Woman, "those are all things I have seen you do, but none of them were enough to make me leave my home here on Spider Rock. There is something else that you did today that made me come and look for you. Tell me what it is and I might allow you to live."

Good Son tried to figure out what she could be referring to, but it was no use. He stayed silent and prayed that his death would come swiftly.

"I abandoned my family," a voice said from behind, "and left my brother to suffer the consequences of my actions."

Good Son's body screamed in pain as he lifted himself up enough to see his brother, Bad Son, who was bloody and bruised from the long climb up the rock.

"That is right, Bad Son," Spider Woman said approvingly.

"You mean, you knew?" asked Good Son, who thought that his deception had been successful right from the start.

"I see everything, Good Son. Did you really think I would not be able to recognize you as well as I could recognize your brother? I did not become a god of your people by being a fool."

This was too much for Good Son to accept. His pain and sacrifice had been for nothing; he had suffered and his brother was still going to die.

"I take it then, Bad Son, that you have come to take his place?"

"Yes," he answered.

"Why should I let someone who deceived me go unpunished?"

"Because the only reason he deceived you was because of his love for me. His is the kindest and gentlest heart this world has ever known, and if you were to eat him, then it would mean a darkness would fall upon this land."

"You say this knowing that it will mean great suffering for yourself? I am a slow eater, and it may take days for you to die. Your agony will be nothing your mortal imagination could ever hope to conceive."

"I know," said Bad Son. "Let my brother go free and I will gladly accept any fate you see fit to bestow upon me."

"That is very noble of you, but tell me this first—how did you get here as quickly as you did? I am much faster than any man and there are few mortals who could reach the top of this rock without my aid, much less with the speed with which you climbed it."

"I don't know, Spider Woman," he admitted. "As I ran and climbed, I felt as though I was being helped and guided by a greater force, but I could not tell you what it was."

"Tell me this then—did it seem as though as you were running with eight legs? Did it feel as though you barely had to touch the rock to make your way up it?"

Bad Son was shocked when he realized where his speed and power had come from. "It was you all along?" he asked.

It was at that moment that the two brothers learned what it looked like when a spider smiled.

"It is true that I originally come to devour you, Bad Son," she explained to them, "but when I saw what your brother was willing to do to save you, I realized that there must be something about you to have earned such devotion. Surely if you were truly wicked then no one would have cared if you lived or died, but that was not the case at all. I decided to test you. I took your brother in your place to see what you would do when you found out. If you had decided to let him die, I would have ended the charade, and you would have suffered more than any mortal has ever experienced, but you raced after us to save him. The journey would have been so arduous that no mortal could have made it without me lending him a part of my power. By following us and climbing Spider Rock, you proved to me that I was wrong to come for you this night, and you deserve to be spared the fate I normally reserve for children who misbehave. And as for you, Good Son, never before have I seen a brother commit such a powerful act of love, and for it, you shall suffer no more."

At that moment all of Good Son's wounds healed and all of his pain disappeared. He was able to stand up and receive a long hug from his grateful brother.

"Now go," said Spider Woman, "and never forget what happened this night."

Both brothers thanked the old god for the gift she had given them. Then they climbed down a web she spun for them and walked back to their home just as the sun was starting to rise. It was a new day.

Whether it was the shock of almost killing his father or the realization that his wicked ways almost had him eaten by a god, Bad Son decided to change his ways. Eventually his family became uncomfortable calling him Bad Son, which now did not match his personality at all, and from that point on they called him As-Good Son and they all lived as happily as life allowed them.

Multnomah Falls

Emptying out on the Oregon side of the Columbia River, the Multnomah Falls were named for a Chinook tribe that lived in the area before they were decimated by an outbreak of malaria in 1830. Their fate adds a note of ironic sadness to this legend, which tells of a Multnomah princess whose sacrifice saved her people from the mysterious plague that had descended upon them just before she was to be married.

Youngest Child dipped her left hand into the water.

It was very cold.

She stood up and looked over the edge of the cliff from which the cold white water fell many feet to the river below.

It would be a short journey—one that ended nearly as fast as it had begun.

She prayed that it would not be a trip taken in vain.

As her feet left the rock at the edge of the cliff, she pretended that she was flying.

She flew all the way into the river.

And in the river she stayed.

*   *   *

The chief of the Multnomah people was once a happy man. He believed that to be a great man required that you have great children who would continue to honor your name long after you had left this phase of life's journey. It was for this reason that he had 10 children, nine sons and one daughter, each one of whom he was proud to call his child; he knew they would never dishonor his memory with their actions.

But times had changed. His people had fought a necessary war with a rival tribe, and in battle all nine of his sons were killed. Though a lasting peace was eventually settled, it had come at the greatest of all possible prices. All that he had left to continue his legacy was his daughter, which would have saddened him greatly were it not for the fact that his daughter was considered the jewel of his people—their greatest source of pride. He affectionately referred to her as Youngest Child, even though she was now a young woman.

The Multnomah people felt as though they had been blessed by the Great Spirit to count her as one of their own, as her great beauty and enormous heart served as proof of all of their virtues.

When it came time for her to marry, her father was very careful about who he chose to become her husband. He knew his people would insist that she only wed a man who was worthy of her—a sentiment with which he wholeheartedly agreed. As word of his search spread across the land, many braves and chiefs from other tribes traveled to the Multnomahs' village to see the famous beauty in person and argue their case for the honor of her hand in marriage.

In the end, her father decided that there was one person whose opinion in this matter he respected more than any other. He asked his only child who she would like to marry and, proving that he knew his daughter well, she answered by naming the one man he had already decided deserved her, the chief of the Clatsop people, the Multnomah's closest allies. It was the most perfect of all possible unions.

Because this was no ordinary marriage but one that would unite two tribes by joining together their two most beloved citizens, the Clatsop and the Multnomah decided to hold a celebration that would last for several days. Each of these days would include an incredible feast and a series of games in which braves from the two tribes would compete for generous prizes.

It was to be the greatest moment in the history of the Multnomah people, but then the sickness descended upon their village.

*   *   *

It started with a single child, but within a few days many people fell ill and at least 12 of them died. The plague hit the Multnomah, and the Clatsop, fearful that it may spread to them, called off the wedding and the celebration.

Knowing that the survival of his people was on the line, Youngest Child's father convened a meeting of the wisest, bravest and oldest members of the tribe and asked them to explain what had caused this plague and what he had to do to stop it.

At first his request for answers was met with only silence. It seemed as though no one had any answer to provide, but then a strained whisper was heard coming from the oldest member of the tribe.

"Someone repeat what he is saying, so that we can all hear it," the chief ordered the brave sitting next to the very old man.

The brave leaned very close to the old man to hear him. As the old man paused for a breath, the brave would quickly repeat what he had heard.

"He says that this is the day he has been waiting for since he was very young and that he is grateful that it has come since it means he can now go on to meet the Great Spirit," the brave told them. He then listened as the old man continued. "He says that when he was still a child, his father, who was the greatest and most powerful of our people's medicine men, told him that in the future the Great Spirit would test our devotion to him by bringing a great sickness to our people and that it would be up to him to tell us what we had to do to stop it."

Everyone held their breaths as the old man whispered to the young brave what needed to be done to end the worst calamity that they had ever faced.

The brave paused before he repeated what he had just heard. He looked down at the old man to make sure that he had not imagined it. He had not.

"He says that to prove our devotion to the Great Spirit, the greatest of us—the person whom we all admire the most in this world—must willingly sacrifice their life by leaping off the cliff that empties water into the river that sustains us."

Everyone gasped when they heard these words. Though they did not say it, they all knew who was chosen by the Great Spirit to make that suicidal leap.

"No!" shouted the chief. "I will not allow it! It is too heavy a price to pay. There must be another way!"

The brave looked down at the old man to see if he had anything else to say, but it was clear that he did not. "The old man is dead," he told everyone.

No one said a word as the weight of their situation fell heavily upon them.

*　　*　　*

What they did not know was that Youngest Child, out of concern for her people, had hidden outside of her father's longhouse so that she could hear what was said at this most important of meetings.

When she heard what needed to be done, she did not hesitate. Her father may think that it was too high a price to pay, but she believed it was a bargain.

Without anyone seeing her she slipped out of the village and ran to the waterfall she had visited many times as a child. Once there she said a prayer to the Great Spirit, dipped a hand into the cold white water and saved her people.

*　　*　　*

The meeting ended without a solution. Everyone left the chief's longhouse agreeing that the price the Great Spirit wanted was too steep, and they would not willingly give up Youngest Child, the source of all their pride, to pay it. They knew that their decision would mean the death of many of them, but they did not care.

That morning they awoke to a great surprise. Those who had been near death the night before were now walking and moving as though they had never been sick at all. All trace of the sickness had vanished across the village—more than that, all trace of *any* sickness had vanished. Those who had been blind could now see. Those who had been deaf could now hear. The lame could walk; the mute could speak. In just one day the Great Spirit had gone from taking the Multnomah to the brink of extinction to making them stronger than they ever had been before.

"How could this be?" asked the chief. "What could have possibly changed the Great Spirit's mind and caused him to bless us so generously?"

The answer to his question came when his daughter could not be found.

No one could find her. She had completely disappeared from the village.

Her father knew then what must have happened. His heart burst with pride over the bravery of his child, who willingly sacrificed her life.

To honor her, he traveled to the waterfall where she had made her heroic leap.

He prayed when he got there. "Great Spirit, I know my daughter is with you because my people are healthy and strong, but she left us without having the chance to say good-bye. Could you please, in your infinite mercy, allow me to see her one last time?"

He then waited for some sign that his request had been heard. It did not take long to come.

Before his eyes, the cool white water, which cascaded off the edge of the cliff, suddenly stopped. Instead, the water flew up into the sky where the many droplets transformed into the shape of his beloved daughter.

"Youngest Child?" he asked the apparition.

Though she could not speak, she smiled to indicate that she was okay and had no regrets about what she had given up for her people.

Knowing this, the chief returned to the village of his people and insisted that the celebration that was originally planned for the wedding continue. The Clatsop tribe, moved by Youngest Child's sacrifice, agreed to take part and everyone honored what they had lost and the miracle that had saved them all.

The chief was finally satisfied that the actions of his children had created a legacy that his people would never forget. He chose to join his daughter in the spirit world and died the day after the celebration had ended.

After his death, many other members of the Multnomah tribe insisted that they, too, had seen the spirit of Youngest Child in the waters of the cliff where she had made her unselfish sacrifice. In time another plague hit the tribe and there were more deaths, but the Great Spirit could no longer be appeased.

Though they are now long gone from this Earth, the Multnomah live on in the waterfall that bears their name and in the spirit of the girl that people claim to see in its waters to this very day.

The Skull

The following story is based on a old legend told in Kansas' Ellis County. Though the legend is vague about the tribal identity of the undead Takaluma, it is most likely that he would have been a member of the Kaw nation.

Henry Wilken was different from most of the other cowboys he knew. For one thing he seldom, if ever, cursed, no matter how much the situation demanded it. He also did his best, no matter where he was, to keep clean. Unlike most of his peers, who always remained oblivious to their own nasty odors, he was quite sensitive about his cleanliness. That was why he usually traveled alongside rivers whenever he could manage it, because this ensured that he was able to bathe as often as he liked. But the major difference between Henry and the other fellows who shared his line of work was that he possessed a college education; he didn't travel anywhere without a couple of books and his personal journal in his riding satchel.

Every now and then, when he wasn't working by himself, some smelly, illiterate cowpuncher would tease Henry's literacy and cleanliness. It was an excuse for the cowpoke to question Henry's manhood, which was a mistake on the cowboy's part. Henry was as good with his fists as he was with his fountain pen and washcloth, and people who insulted him would end up flat on their backs with either a broken nose or some missing teeth. Henry was smart, but he definitely wasn't a sissy.

Luckily for his knuckles, his fists wouldn't be required on this particular job, since it required him to work alone picking off some pesky coyotes that were causing trouble for the local farmers in Ellis County. These varmints seemed to share his enthusiasm for fresh water by making their homes in areas along the Saline River.

He liked working alone and appreciated how it allowed him to enjoy his own thoughts, without having to listen to some old-timer wheezing, belching and farting beside him. That was another way he was different from most other cowboys—he avoided foods that made him gassy.

He also liked the quiet nights when he could sit down and write in his journal without anyone interrupting to ask him what he was writing about. Such questions inevitably led to the kind of meandering conversations around a campfire had by bored men looking to pass the time before they fell asleep.

Despite his solitude and the creative freedom that came with it, his first few journal entries differed little from what he usually wrote when he was on a regular job; nothing had happened so far that was worth documenting.

That soon changed.

*   *   *

January 23rd, 1879

When Hamlet spoke to the ghost of his father, he was able to describe the experience to his best friend, Horatio, who tells the prince that he finds the thought of the encounter to be very strange. Hamlet's answer is to tell his friend: "There are more things in Heaven and Earth, Horatio, than are dreamt of in your philosophy."

Until this day I had never realized just how smart this advice truly is. I am still not sure if what happened this afternoon really occurred, or if I dreamed it and have yet to awaken. If it did happen, then these words are actually being set for prosperity, and will still be here for me to read tomorrow. Then let me admit now that the limits of my philosophy have been forever expanded, and I shall never again be surprised by the potential strangeness of this world or the next.

I have to first start with what happened at the beginning. When I awoke to see the sun rising in the sky, this day appeared to be no different than any other. Yes, it was warmer than the winter weather usually allows; otherwise, it was the same mediocre existence. The river was still too cold to bathe in, so I had to make do with washing myself with some water that I warmed over the fire. I finished eating the rest of the rabbit, which I shot the night before, for breakfast and then went out in search of the last two coyotes I had been hired to find and kill.

While the other four had been easy to track and shoot, this final pair was proving to be of much wilier stock. As I searched for them, I began to notice that the area around me seemed oddly devoid of natural life. This concerned me not only because it appeared that my quarry was nowhere to be found, but also because it meant I might have to make do with the last of the dried beef in my satchel for dinner that night, a prospect I wasn't much looking forward to. Were it not for the sight of a single roadrunner (which I left alone since the scant meat it would have provided was not worth taking its life) I would have gone the whole day without seeing a single animal in my midst.

156 Native American Ghost Stories

The last time I saw something like this happen, a fire was traveling through a prairie toward the forest and the animals had scattered so quickly to escape from its flames. But today there was no smoke in the sky and there was no other sign of any danger that the animals might have sensed before me. There was, as far as I could tell, no natural explanation for what I was observing, but I soon discovered that I was wrong in part. There was a natural explanation for the phenomenon—just not one dreamt of in my philosophy.

I had gone to the river to refill my canteen when I saw a man approaching me in the distance. As far as he was, I could tell that he was an Indian by his clothes and the way he walked. I thought maybe he would be able to tell me where the animals had gone, so I waited where I stood as he approached me.

As he grew closer I realized that something was not right. A foul scent filled the air and brought tears to my eyes. I have a sensitive nose, and I began to choke as this heavy odor filled my lungs. It was, I sensed to my horror, the smell of death. The man who was approaching me was not of this earth and bore the marks of someone who had recently arisen from his own grave.

My instincts told me to run, but something about the haunted figure told me that I had nothing to fear. He would not harm me. The closer he came the better I could see how his time under the ground had robbed him of his innate humanity. His face was incomplete, as parts of it had been long eaten by the denizens of the Earth's soil. He had no nose or eyes, and his cold, leathery skin was stretched too tight against his yellowing bones. He was the most horrible figure that I had ever seen, and there was something about his deformity that I could not help but find fascinating. I wondered for a moment if he would even be capable of speaking, given how decomposed he was, but then I realized that the same supernatural force that allowed him to walk would undoubtedly allow him to speak as well. The question was whether or not I would understand him. I speak no other language than English and would not be able to communicate with him if he knew no other tongue than his own.

As it turned out, this was not a problem.

"You there," the dead man said with a voice that was wet from things I did not want to imagine living in his chest, "where is it?" He clearly assumed that I was in possession of something he desired. "Where did you put it?" he asked again, but since I did not know what he was talking about I could not provide a satisfactory answer. I told him as much, but he did not seem to believe me.

"Someone stole it," he told me. "They dug it out of the ground and I cannot rest until I get it back."

I decided at that moment to see if I could change the subject and perhaps discover what was causing this bizarre situation to occur. "Do you have a name?" I asked.

For a moment he went silent and still, as if he was reaching deep back into his mind for the memory of who he once was. "I believe they called me Takaluma," he finally answered, "but it has been so long since I've been called anything."

"And what is that you are looking for?" I asked.

"His skull. They took his skull."

"Whose skull?"

"My father's. He was the chief of our people."

"And what was his name?"

He paused again, but instead of answering me I could see a wave of sorrow pass through his rotting body. "I cannot remember," he finally admitted. "It has been so long and my mind is full of many holes."

I had to stop myself from shuddering at the notion that this was both literally and figuratively true.

"But names matter not," the dead man insisted, "I must find my father's skull. It is a great insult to our people for it to be taken and not returned."

"Of course," I said. I sympathized with him, but then he said something that made me go pale and turned my blood cold.

"If I do not get it back soon, then more will rise."

"More?"

"My father's people will rise and all together we will search for that which has been taken from us."

I knew then that I had to appease the dead man and tell him that I would find his father's skull for him. If I didn't, the consequence would be an army of the dead rising up from their graves to wreak havoc on this land.

"I will give you until the next full moon," said the man who was once named Takaluma when he heard my promise.

That gives me four days.

I am tired now and must rest. When I wake up tomorrow, I shall open this journal, and if I see these words, then I will know that what I saw today was not a dream, and that I cannot rest again until my mission is complete.

*   *   *

January 24th, 1879

It was not a dream. Everything I saw yesterday was real. My mind is moving too fast for me to write anything more.

*   *   *

January 25th, 1879

I am very close to finding the skull. I cannot think about what will happen if I do not.

*   *   *

January 25th, 1879

It can't be done. Unless I think of something else to do, the dead will rise tomorrow night.

*   *   *

January 26th 1879

I have a plan. In just a few hours I will discover if it worked or not.

*   *   *

February 21st, 1879

It has been nearly a month, but it took until today before they agreed to give me my journal. I told them that without it I would not write the confession they wanted from me. They have made good on their end of the deal, so I must make good on mine. Here, now, is my confession.

I will not take the time to go over my strange encounter with the dead man named Takaluma, since I describe it in detail in the pages that precede this one. I will say that the meeting chilled me to my very marrow—not because the dead man himself was so terrifying, but because he had told me that he would soon be followed by an army of living corpses. How do you fight against those who cannot be killed? I knew they would not rest until they received the satisfaction they desired. Who knew how many people would die in the chaos that followed—not just at the hands of the walking dead, but from the panic that would naturally prevail throughout the state and maybe even the entire country itself?

After I woke up the next day and discovered in my diary that I had not dreamed the whole encounter, I got on my horse and rode to Ellis County. Takaluma had told me that someone had dug up his father's skull, which meant that one or more of the nearby farms had to have been built on an Indian burial ground. Based on the books I had seen in his library, I knew that a farmer who had once hired me—a fellow named Caldicott—had a strong interest in local history. Of all the folks I knew, he would probably have the best idea if this was the case and which farms were the most likely prospects.

But when I arrived at his farm and asked him what I needed to know, he became agitated and unpleasant. He asked me why an ignorant cowboy would want to know such a thing. I was just about to tell him when I hesitated, certain that if I told him the truth he would think I was insane.

The truth is, as I sit here and write this, I cannot help but wonder if I am insane. Based on my actions alone it would be impossible to come to any other conclusion, but if all a man truly has is his ability to perceive, then I must assume that what I did was the product of a rational mind. I suppose it does not really matter, since either way I am doomed.

I had to think quickly of a reasonable excuse for my interest in this ghoulish area of history, but rather than fail me my mind came up with a premise that served me better than I could have dreamed.

"I know someone," I told Caldicott, "who has an interest in bizarre antiques. He told me that if I were to ever hear word of someone excavating bones from an Indian burial ground, he would make it worth my while."

At once Caldicott went from being angry and suspicious to becoming my closest ally in the world. With a large grin on his face, he told me that it was his farm that was built on the Indian burial ground, and one of his farmhands had uncovered a skull just a week before while tilling a patch of soil.

"Like you, I knew a man who had expressed an interest in this sort of unusual item and I was able to sell it to him for $100. I have a whole field full of these bones, and I would be willing to pay you a percentage of what I earned if you were able to bring me people interested in buying them."

I did not ask him if any of his farmhands had noticed a patch of freshly turned up earth that appeared mysteriously in his lucrative field, nor did I warn him that more patches like this would result if he continued with his fiendish trade. But I did inquire about the identity of the man who had bought the unearthed skull.

"He's another farmer, like myself, named Meyer. He lives about 30 miles down the road."

I talked to him some more after that so I would not arouse his suspicions, but having gotten the information I left as soon as I could. Ten minutes later I finally got my chance. I started racing to Meyer's farm, but the clouds in the night sky obscured the moonlight and made it far too dark to see. My horse refused to go any farther, so I decided to rest until sunrise, which was just a few hours away. I made a quick note in my diary, and then I slept until I felt the touch of daylight upon me.

With the sun in the sky, I got back on my horse and rode to Meyer's farm. There, I met a man who was just as vile and corrupt as Caldicott. He told me that he was no longer in possession of the skull, having sold it to an antiquities dealer for $250. I asked him where I could find this dealer and was devastated to hear that he was, at that moment, on a train to New York City.

The skull was, as far as I was concerned, gone. There was no way I could retrieve it before Takaluma's deadline passed. I spent the rest of the day wallowing in despair. As I saw it, I could either leave and let everyone deal with Takaluma's army of the dead on their own, or I could attempt to devise a new solution for my problem—one that would satisfy the dead man enough that he would return to his grave.

Of course my first instinct was to find another skull and tell Takaluma that it was the one that belonged to his father, but I feared what might happen if such a ruse failed. Surely a power that was strong enough to animate the dead could not be deceived by so simple a trick.

The day turned to night, and I could not sleep as I attempted to think of what I could do. It was only at sunrise that it occurred to me that Takaluma might be convinced to accept a reasonable trade for what had been taken from his people. If I could not return his father's skull to him, maybe he might accept the skulls of those that had stolen it.

I know they will call what I did next the act of a madman, and I cannot disagree, but I was desperate to spare other innocent lives the pain I was certain they would suffer if I did nothing instead.

I rode back to Meyer's farm, and before he could say a word to me, I shot him with my rifle. I then found an ax and cut off his head, which I stashed into a burlap sack. After that, I rode back to Caldicott's farm and asked him to tell me which of his farmhands found the skull. Then I shot Caldicott, cut off his head and placed it in the sack. I went outside and found the farmhand and killed him before he had time to even suspect what my intentions really were. I collected his head and rode as fast as I could to the spot where I had encountered Takaluma.

I waited there for several long hours. As each hour passed, I feared that I had murdered three men for nothing, but then I saw the familiar figure of the rotting Indian walking toward me.

"I have given you until the full moon," he told me. "Have you found my father's skull?"

"No," I answered him honestly, "but I did not come here empty-handed. In my search for what was stolen from your father, I discovered a scheme to sell the remains of your people to men who delight in collecting strange things. If they were to continue, then, much more than your father's skull would have been taken from your people. That is why I hope that my gifts will appease you and keep you from bringing up an army of the dead to continue in your search."

"What kind of gifts could possibly do that?" asked Takaluma.

"This kind," I told him, as I emptied the contents of the burlap sack onto the ground at his feet. "These belong to the men who stole your father's skull, and they would have continued to rob your graves until there was nothing left to take."

Takaluma took a moment to consider this and then picked up the head of Caldicott.

"I am appeased," he told me. "I will call no one else to aid in my search, but I cannot rest until I have found my father's skull."

"Try looking in New York City," I said. "I doubt that anyone will even notice you over there."

He then took the three gifts I had given him and left me alone at the edge of the Saline River.

I knew that if I was not already a wanted man, it would only be a matter of time before I became one. I hid out as long as I could, but I did not have the supplies that I needed. One week ago they caught me and wanted me to confess before they slipped the noose around my neck. This is my confession.

The noose awaits.

*   *   *

Henry Wilkins was hanged on February 21, 1879. It is not known if the skull of Takaluma's father was ever found.

Thunder Without A Storm

The Kiowa were a nomadic people, who, by the time of the first European settlers, lived mostly in the areas that would eventually become Texas, Oklahoma and New Mexico. The Kiowa depended upon horses for hunting and for battle, so without horses their lifestyle would be seriously jeopardized. The following story deals with the legend of the Phantom Horses of Palo Duro Canyon.

Wallace was surprised when his mother told him how he was going to spend his spring break vacation, and not in a good way.

"Are you kidding me?" he asked her disbelievingly, hoping that she was acting out of character and had just told him a rare joke. "You can't be serious."

"Yes I can," she said. "Your grandfather is going to pick you up tomorrow, so I suggest you start packing now. Remember to bring your toothbrush; just because you'll be out in the wilderness is no excuse for poor dental hygiene."

"I'm not going," he told her as he crossed his arms in bold defiance. He had just turned 15 and felt he was now man enough to take such stands. He was wrong.

"What was that?" his mother asked with a slight grin evident in the corner of her lips—she thought his newfound bravery was almost as adorable as it was misguided.

"I told you, I'm not going. Me and Rod made plans to spend the week unlocking all of the characters in *Shinto Monkey Fighter III*. There are 124 of them."

"So let me get this straight," she said as she stared at him, "you would rather waste away your week playing a video game with a friend you see every day than go out camping with your grandfather who you only see a couple times out of the year."

"Yes," he answered with hesitation. It wasn't the kind of question he would ever have to think about.

"Fine," she said in a tone that clearly indicated that it was not fine and that she was about to do something on the harsh side of extreme, "if that is how you want to spend your spring break, I won't stop you."

"But…" sighed Wallace under his breath, knowing a big condition had to be on its way. He was not disappointed.

"But," she continued, "after the week is up you will be grounded for the rest of the year and I will give away all of your video games to a family with a child who isn't a spoiled, ungrateful brat."

Her words turned Wallace pale. "You're joking, right?" he asked.

"Wallace, you've known me your entire life—when have I ever had a sense of humor?"

"Fine," he said angrily, his tone clearly indicating that the situation was not fine and that he was going to resent this act of extreme cruelty for his entire life. "I'll go camping with Granddad. But don't expect me to like it."

His mother smiled and patted his cheek in that way only a mother could ever get away with. "Don't forget your toothbrush," she reminded him.

*   *   *

There were three reasons why Wallace didn't want to go out camping with his grandfather. The first was that he had been genuinely psyched about spending the week playing his favorite video game with his best friend, and it came as a crushing disappointment that it wasn't going to happen (at least until summer vacation started). The second was that he genuinely hated camping, being the type of person who couldn't comprehend how people lived before the invention of indoor plumbing and cable television.

The third reason—the one he would never admit to anyone out loud, but which was the one that made him the most reluctant to go—was that there was something about his grandfather that he found embarrassing to deal with.

He was afraid to clearly state what that something was, but in his most honest moments, he could not ignore what really bothered him: his grandfather embarrassed him because he was *too Indian*.

His grandfather was a full-blooded Kiowa and he was very proud of his heritage. Unfortunately he had never been able to instill this same pride in his son, Robert—Wallace's father—who felt more comfortable adopting the ways of his British mother. This drove a wedge between the two of them for most of Wallace's life, which ended when Robert died in car accident.

Devastated by the loss and the end of any hope for reconciliation that came with it, Wallace's grandfather decided that he would not make the same mistake again. With his daughter-in-law's blessing he began making semiannual visits to Oklahoma City to spend time with Wallace, who he soon discovered was completely ignorant of his Kiowa ancestry. Much to Wallace's dismay, he made every effort to correct this problem by attempting to teach his grandson as much as he could about his ancestors' history during his brief visits.

Wallace suspected, correctly as it turned out, that his grandfather had more in mind for this trip than a few days sleeping in a tent and sitting around a campfire, and the last thing he wanted was to spend his week away from school receiving another kind of education. His mother may have found a way to force him to go, but there was nothing she could do that would make him listen to the old man or care about anything he had to say.

*   *   *

As shocking as the news of the camping trip was, it was nothing compared to what Wallace's grandfather did when he arrived at the house at nine o'clock that morning.

"Where are your bags?" he asked his grandson after the most cursory of greetings.

"Right there," Wallace said sullenly pointing to the duffle bag and knapsack that he packed to make the trip.

His grandfather turned in the small foyer and looked down at the two bags. He bent over and opened them and started to inspect their contents.

"What are you doing?" asked Wallace, who couldn't believe he was actually witnessing such a blatant disrespect for his privacy.

"It is important that we do not bring anything that might distract us from our surroundings," his grandfather explained. "Like this," he said as he pulled out Wallace's portable video game system, "and this," as he removed his grandson's MP3 player.

"No way!" Wallace protested. "What am I supposed to do for a whole week without my PSP and iPod?"

"Learn something," his grandfather answered back. "I can't find any books in here—you didn't pack any?"

"No. Why would I?"

Instead of answering his question, his grandfather just looked very sad. He continued rifling through Wallace's bags until he was certain that all they contained were his clothes and toiletries.

"Okay," he said as he stood back up and handed Wallace the two bags, "we can go now."

"Whatever," Wallace sighed under his breath, his eyes rolling at maximum petulance. "Where are we going, anyway?" he asked, hoping it wouldn't be too far a drive—he hated long car trips.

"Texas," his grandfather answered him. "The Palo Duro Canyon State Park."

"Where's that?"

"Not far from Amarillo. It's about a five-hour drive, give or take an hour or two. Depends on how many state troopers are out on the road," he joked.

Wallace, however, did not see the humor in this. "So I'm supposed to spend five hours in a car without any video games or music to pass the time?" he said, as if the concept was beyond the imagination of any intelligent human being.

"It'll pass quicker than you think."

"Why? Are you going to tell me a bunch of stories about my ancestors?" Wallace asked wearily.

"No, I have the latest Stephen King book on tape and we can listen to it during the drive. I hear it's a lot scarier than his last one."

"You like Stephen King?"

His grandfather smiled. "I like a lot of things. I am a man of many tastes."

"And they all taste bad," Wallace mumbled under his breath.

"You should know," his grandfather warned him, "that I have excellent hearing for a man my age, and I spent years working with men who never spoke clearly a day in their life, so it might be in your best interest to keep nasty remarks like that to yourself."

Wallace couldn't tell if the old man was bluffing or not, so from that moment on he decided that he wasn't going to say anything during the entire trip. Instead of responding with a smart-ass quip, he just picked up his bags and followed his grandfather out of the front door.

*   *   *

His grandfather's pickup truck had to be at least 20 years old, but you wouldn't know it to look at it. He had taken such good care of it over the years that only its mid-80s design details betrayed its age. Wallace, who was usually only interested in cars when they appeared in racing games, had to admit that it made for a pretty sweet ride. It wasn't totally pimped out or anything, but it was still far cooler than he had any right to expect it to be.

This was just as true for the truck's interior as it was for its exterior. As he stepped into it, Wallace could tell that not a single fast food meal had ever been eaten inside and that nary a piece of trash had ever touched its floor. It was all so pristine that he forgot his vow of silence and commented on it.

"Wow," he said with obvious awe, "you must be really anal about this truck."

"Excuse me?" asked his grandfather.

"It just looks like no one has ever driven it," Wallace explained. "It makes me paranoid that you'll freak out at me if my butt leaves too big an indentation in the seat cover."

His grandfather laughed, which surprised him. "Take a look at this," he said with pride.

Wallace bent over in his seat to see the odometer at 923,346 miles. "Holy crap!" he marveled. "How did you do that? Mom's last car died before she even got 90,000 clicks on it. You're only 77,000 miles away from going back to zero!"

"My father taught me many valuable things," his grandfather explained, "but the one lesson of his that I appreciated the most was to treat everything in this world, no matter what it was, with the respect it deserved. This old truck has been very good to me over the years. Without it, I might have spent my retirement sitting on a couch like so many other folks do these days, so it only seems fair to me that I do right by it as well."

"But it's just a truck," said Wallace. "It's just doing what it's been built to do."

"That doesn't mean you have the right to show it no gratitude. I suspect that the reason your mother's car died so quickly was because she took it for granted and never changed its oil in time or listened to it when it started making a coughing sound. If she had, I bet it would still be running today."

"Is this supposed to be some mystical Indian lesson?" asked Wallace.

"No," answered his grandfather, "it's just a good way to not have to buy a new car every five years."

*   *   *

True to his word, Wallace's grandfather filled in the awkward silence between them by playing an audiobook by the famous Master of Horror. Wallace soon found himself hypnotized by Stephen King's New England accent, which was one he had never heard before. Almost against his will the time passed by quickly, which made it difficult for him to resent it.

They stopped only once, to get some gas and buy snacks (which were consumed before they got back into the truck), and since the highway was miraculously free of troopers for virtually the entire trip, they were able to make good time by traveling at a speed that was over the limit without being reckless.

It was mid-afternoon when they drove into the park. There they entered a small cabin to pay for the campsite Wallace's grandfather had reserved for the night. Inside, Wallace found a brochure that described the various facilities that were available to visitors. He visibly perked up when he saw that the park had three cabins that were equipped with bathrooms and air conditioning. He tried to convince his grandfather that he wouldn't be so miserable if they stayed at one of these spots, but even if his grandfather had been willing to change his plans (and pay the extra $618 it would cost to switch to the best of the three cabins) it wouldn't have mattered because the cabins were already reserved. The same was true for the four much smaller "Cow Camp Cabins," which were much less luxurious but still preferable to sleeping outside in a tent.

Wallace continued reading the brochure while his grandfather was driving to their campsite, which was in one of the park's two "Developed Primitive Areas." He really didn't like that word "primitive," and he liked the name of the site they were driving to—Cactus—even less. According to the pamphlet, all he could expect to find when they got there was a table, a shade shelter, a fire ring, an undefined water source and a *two-mile* walk to the nearest indoor restroom facilities.

This alone would have completed Wallace's mental picture of what Hell looked like, but the fact that he was also going to be denied the tools necessary for his survival (the previously jettisoned PSP and iPod), the result was a concentric circle of suffering that would have given Dante himself the screaming heebie-jeebies.

The look of utter anguish on his face was so evident his grandfather couldn't stop himself from trying to say something that might make it go away. "Aw, cheer up. I bet there are plenty of kids who would love to spend a week out camping in a place as beautiful as this."

"Find one and I'd be happy to swap places with them," Wallace muttered unhappily.

"You know what you're so afraid of?" asked his grandfather.

"No, please tell me," Wallace answered sarcastically.

"You're afraid of what's lurking down inside your own head."

"What?"

"It's true. Why else would you be so miserable about the prospect of facing a week without all of your gizmos and gadgets? I'll tell you why—because they are what distract you from the thoughts you'd prefer not to think about."

"Since when did you become Dr. Phil?"

"Hey, as far as bald white guys go, he's not a bad fellow to listen to every now and then."

Wallace decided not to encourage the old man, so he kept his mouth shut and stared out his side window as they drove toward the "Cactus" campsite. What he saw really didn't match up with his idea of what a national park was supposed to look like. Having spent his youth watching old Yogi Bear reruns on the Cartoon Network, he had naturally assumed that all parks were densely wooded areas filled with thousands of trees behind which one could lurk while on the hunt for "pic-a-nic" baskets. Palo Duro wasn't like that—at all. It was a desert canyon filled with brush and cacti and very few trees, and its most discernable feature was the red rock spires that twisted their way out of the ground.

"Did you know they call this place the Grand Canyon of Texas?" asked his grandfather, breaking the brief silence.

"Yeah, it says that here on the brochure."

"Personally I think that's overselling it a bit. I've been to a lot of places around this world, and I've yet to see anything that can reasonably be compared to what they have there in Arizona. Still, I guess they have to sell it to people somehow."

"Have you camped here before?" asked Wallace, who was mildly surprised by his own curiosity.

"Just twice. Once when I was your age and once with your father."

"I can't picture my dad out in a place like this," said Wallace as he continued to look out his window.

"Neither could he," said his grandfather.

*   *   *

Wallace was horrified when they finally drove into their campsite, which was the last one in the section and, therefore, the farthest away from public restrooms. He shuddered at the thought that every time he felt the call of nature he would either be required to walk two miles to get to the nearest flushable toilet, or ask his grandfather for a ride. Inevitably, he knew that he had to consider the third option.

"Where are we supposed to sleep?" Wallace had visions of people on reality shows like *Survivor* sleeping on the ground beside tiny, pitiful campfires.

His grandfather sensed his fear and allowed himself a quiet chuckle at the boy's expense. "I have a tent," he told him. "I don't want to get rained on any more than you do."

This did little to ease Wallace's fears, as he imagined them sharing a tiny pup tent made out of green cloth and tree branches. It was only when he started helping his grandfather set it up that he realized his situation wasn't as dire as he thought it would be—at least as far as shelter was concerned. It took them half an hour to get the tent fully erected, which normally would have taken 15 minutes, but Wallace's "help" slowed the process down, and when Wallace walked into it, he had to admit that, as far as tents went, it was pretty sweet.

"This thing is bigger than my room," he said. "No, it's bigger than *my mom's* room."

His grandfather smiled. "I like it. Keeps the rain off your head and lets you stretch out your feet."

"And play a few games of indoor football," added Wallace.

"You know, you can be a pretty funny guy when you're not being a sarcastic jerk."

"Uh, thanks," said Wallace, who was sure that there was a compliment lurking in there somewhere. "What do we do next?"

"I don't know about you, but I could definitely eat."

"Does that mean we have to go hunting or something?"

"I doubt the park warden would appreciate that," said his grandfather. "It might be better if we just ate the food I packed in the cooler."

Something about his mistaken assumption made Wallace blush with embarrassment. "Uh…okay," he said, wishing that at some point he would say something that wouldn't make him sound like such a dumbass. "Are we going to need to build a fire?"

"I tell you what, how about you get on that while I unpack the rest of our stuff."

"Okay. How am I supposed to do it? Do you want me to rub two sticks together?"

"No, I'd prefer to have a fire sometime before we leave, so it's probably best that you use these." His grandfather took a book of matches from out of his pocket and threw them over to him.

"Right. So I guess I'll need to find some dry wood and grass and stuff like that?"

"Probably wouldn't hurt."

Wallace nodded and walked out of the tent to look for flammable debris around the campsite. As he gathered every branch and piece of stray moss that came his way, his grandfather unloaded several bags and coolers from the back of the truck. He took his time, having decided that he was tired of constantly looking like an idiot and wanted to do a good job. By the time he returned to the fire pit with a full armload of combustible material, his grandfather was sitting on a plastic folding chair waiting for him.

The old man didn't say a word as Wallace laid down the branches and dried moss and tried to set them aflame with one of his matches. He had no problem getting them to burn, but he couldn't get the fire to last for more than a few seconds. As he grew more and more frustrated, he looked over to his grandfather, waiting for the old man to supply him with the wisdom of thousands of years of Kiowa fire-building techniques, but he didn't say a word. Instead, he just watched on as Wallace tried all of the little tricks he had seen folks on TV use.

Finally, after 45 minutes, he was able to create a strong, steady flame. The last time he had felt such a sense of accomplishment was when he finally finished the final level of *Ultimate Phantom Dragon III*, by far the hardest video game he had ever played. He looked up at his grandfather, and the old man smiled and laughed.

"About time. I was about to throw some gasoline on there just so I wouldn't have to watch you struggle anymore. I'm glad I didn't though—I don't like the way that stuff makes the hot dogs taste."

"We're having hot dogs?"

"Of course! You have to have hot dogs your first night out camping—it's the law!"

"For re—" Wallace started to ask, but he thought better of it.

*   *   *

It took Wallace three tries before he managed to roast a hot dog without burning it charcoal black. He was shocked by how good it tasted—far better than any other hot dog he could remember. He liked it so much that he immediately started cooking another one.

"If you keep going through wieners like that, I'm going to have to pick up more supplies sooner than I thought," his grandfather said with a chuckle.

"I'm sorry," Wallace said with a mouthful of hot dog still sitting half-chewed in his mouth.

"Don't be. I'm just glad I found something you like to eat. I know how fussy you kids can be when it comes to food."

"I'm not a kid," Wallace protested. "I'm 15 and I like a lot of different kind of foods. I eat sushi all the time. Have you?"

"I tried it when I was in Japan. Can't say that I cared for it, though. It wasn't so much the taste, I just didn't like the way the raw fish felt in my mouth."

"You've been to Japan?"

"A long time ago, back when I was in the Air Force."

"You were in the Air Force?"

"Didn't you know that?"

"Why would I?" asked Wallace.

"I don't know. I just figured it would have come up before."

"Were you a fighter pilot?"

"No, nothing that exciting. I was a mechanic. I worked mostly on big transport planes."

"Did you fight in any wars?"

"No, I just missed going to Korea and I got out before Vietnam."

"Oh," said Wallace, disappointed that he wasn't going to hear any good gory combat stories. "So nothing much interesting happened to you then?"

"I wouldn't say that. If I hadn't been in the Air Force, you wouldn't be here today."

"Really?"

"Definitely. If it wasn't for the Air Force I never would have spent the summer of 1959 in England, and I wouldn't have met your grandmother. How much do you know about her?"

"Not a lot. I've seen pictures of her, though. I always thought she was very beautiful."

"She was. She most definitely was. In fact she was so beautiful that I avoided her for the whole first month she came into my life."

"How come?"

"Because I was just 20 years old and still thought of myself as an ignorant Indian from a no-name small town in Oklahoma. I was afraid that if I went near her she might start talking to me, and I was so mesmerized by her that I couldn't say anything and would have looked like a complete jackass. She was working as a barmaid at the pub we all used to hang out at, and whenever she was in for that first month, I had to have other people go up to the bar to order for me."

"How'd you end up talking to her?"

"I was sitting alone in a corner nursing a beer and she came up to me, sat down and started asking me questions."

"Like what?"

"She wanted to know if I was really an Indian and what tribe I was from. When I told her I was a Kiowa, she wanted to know all about our history and customs. It turned out she was studying history when she wasn't working at the pub, and she was fascinated by stories of the American West. I was the first honest-to-goodness Native American she had ever met. She told me that she kept wishing that I'd come over and talk to her at the bar, but I never did, so she decided to come in to see me on her day off. She caught me so off guard when she went on and started asking questions that I completely forgot to remember how nervous she had made me before."

"That's cool."

"It was more than that. Back then it was tough being a minority in the military—I suspect it probably still is. I had to deal with morons everyday who insisted on calling me names like Big Chief, Running Bear and Injun Joe. Don't get me wrong, I got to know a lot of good folks and some of them are friends of mine to this day, but sometimes I felt very alone, away from my family and culture, surrounded by people who thought it was funny to make Indian war cries every time I walked into a room. The day your grandmother started talking to me was the first time I realized that I wasn't alone, just unique. There was no one else around like me and I had to take pride in the fact that I was special, no matter what anyone else said or did to try and make me feel ashamed of who I was. Because of her, I started standing up for myself and soon no one was whooping or hollering and calling me 'Injun' when I came into a room."

"It always seemed stupid to me to hate or make fun of a person because of their race," said Wallace, "when chances are if you took the time to get to know them you could find a much better reason to hate and make fun of them."

Hearing this, his grandfather started laughing. "That's very funny. Did you think of it yourself?"

"No, I heard a comedian say it on TV."

"It's definitely true, whoever said it."

"Did you and Grandma start dating right away?"

"We didn't get a chance to. I got shipped to Japan the next day. I was pretty sure that we'd never see each other again."

"So what happened?"

"She sent me a letter. She was able to find out where I was stationed from one of the Air Force regulars at the pub and she wrote me. I must have made a real impression on her. Soon we were sending each other a letter a week. I continued going wherever they said they needed me, hoping each time it would be a place where I could steal away for a few days and see her again. It took a year, but it finally happened. I got stationed at a base in France and got a few days worth of leave. After being pen pals for all of that time, we finally had our first date. We got engaged six months later and I married her a year after that, the day after I got out of the force. She moved with me back to Oklahoma and we had your dad two years after that."

"Why didn't you and he get along?"

"Mostly because we were too much alike and too different at the same time. He inherited my stubbornness and pride, but he saw the world very differently than I did, so when he grew old enough to have opinions of his own, every conversation we had turned into a fight."

"How did he see the world?"

"Well, you lived with him for most of your life, so you should know that as well as anyone."

"I guess. Mostly all I remember is him being worried about money."

"Sometimes people can't appreciate what they have in the present because they're too afraid of what may happen in the future."

"Yeah, that was Dad." Wallace looked up and noticed that the sky had turned dark. "Wow," he said, "it sure did turn dark really quickly. I didn't even notice the sunset."

"We should head on into the tent and get some sleep," his grandfather said. "It's been a long day."

*   *   *

Wallace had no idea what to expect that first night in the tent. He had been worried that his back might get sore sleeping on the floor, which was only a thin layer of nylon between him and the ground, but to his relief his grandfather produced two inflatable mattresses for them to sleep on. They took turns pumping them up, which was oddly enjoyable even if it did feel uncomfortably close to hard work. When both mattresses were fully inflated, Wallace was surprised to discover that it was almost as comfortable as his own bed. Within a couple of minutes he fell asleep, and as the night continued he started to dream.

And for the first time, his dreams were not filled with amorous fantasies involving the popular girls at his school or the attractive young women he saw everyday on television, nor were there thrilling adventures in which he saved the world riding on a motorcycle or jet. That first night in the tent, he dreamed of only one thing—his father.

But what he saw was not the man he knew, but rather his father when he was his age. He was tall like Wallace was, but he looked handsome and young. Wallace was so captivated by this image of his young father that it took him a moment to notice where he was and what was around him. His father was in the canyon not far from where he and his grandfather were and he was surrounded by horses: there were at least a thousand of them, each one more beautiful than the last.

He tried to speak to his father, but this was a dream where all he could do was watch and nothing more. It was then that he noticed his grandfather, also much younger, standing by one of the horses and petting its thick mane of hair.

"Come here, son," Wallace heard him say, "come and pet this fine animal."

"No," answered Wallace's father. His voice was filled with anger. "There is nothing there. There is no animal."

"But it is right here in front of you," said Wallace's grandfather. "How can you not see it?"

"Because it's not there!"

"But look around you, we are surrounded by them!"

"We're surrounded by nothing," his father said, and to prove it, he started to walk forward. "We're in a canyon looking for spirits that do not exist." To Wallace's amazement, his father passed through the horses like they were composed only of wind and air.

"Why can't you see them?" asked Wallace's grandfather, his voice breaking with frustration and despair.

"Because they do not exist!" his son shouted at him. His words echoed through the canyon and spooked the herd, causing them to fade away as if they had never really been there.

"Want some breakfast?" a voice piped in.

"Huh?" Wallace heard himself say. After a second he realized he was no longer dreaming. He opened his eyes and saw his grandfather standing above him. It was morning.

"Do you want some breakfast?" his grandfather asked again. "I can whip up some bacon and eggs, if you're hungry."

"Yes, please," Wallace answered him. It was odd seeing his grandfather as an old man again after seeing the younger version of him in the dream.

"How'd you sleep?"

"Good," said Wallace. "I can't believe how comfortable this mattress is."

His grandfather laughed. "I'll say. Sure beats sleeping on the ground."

*   *   *

Wallace didn't tell his grandfather about his dream.

Instead the two of them spent the day walking around the park, getting to know each other better. Wallace's grandfather told more stories about his days in the Air Force and his years working as a mechanic at the garage he opened when he returned to Oklahoma, while Wallace talked about his favorite subjects in school (math and biology) and his plans for the future (either he would become a game designer or win the lottery, whichever happened first).

When they got back to their campsite, his grandfather lent him a book to read. He worried a bit when he saw that it was a spy thriller set during the Second World War, but it turned out that he had played enough WWII video games to understand most of the historical references. After the first chapter he became so engrossed in the story that he completely forgot that he could have been playing a game or listening to some music instead.

That night he fell asleep just as easily as he had the night before and he dreamed the same dream. It once again ended with the herd of horses fading away, unable to fight the power of Wallace's father's insistence that they did not exist.

The days passed and the boredom that Wallace had been dreading never seemed to come. He came to realize just how cool his grandfather really was and how fun it could be to disconnect from the world. That Thursday night, the last before they left for home, he told his grandfather all of this, and the old man was very moved to hear it.

"At least I got one of the things I wanted," he told Wallace. "And I suppose that was more than I could ask for."

"What else did you want?" asked Wallace.

"It doesn't matter. I just thought we might relive something that happened when my father took me here back when I was your age. I tried to share the experience with your father, but it never happened. I had hoped that this time it would be different."

"What was it?"

"It's not the sort of thing you can describe. If it had happened, you would have known it."

Wallace felt bad that he hadn't been able to give his grandfather the experience he had wanted, but he was happy to have spent the week with him. That night was the first he had trouble getting to sleep. He didn't want to sleep because he didn't want this last day to end, but eventually he couldn't fight it any longer and he drifted off into a deep sleep, in which he dreamed the same dream from the past four nights.

But this time the dream was different. The horses, who had previously been so calm and docile, were now riled and angry. And the cause of their distress appeared to be his father's refusal to acknowledge their existence. The horses began to whine and snort as if they were offended by his denial of them.

"Why can't you see them?" asked Wallace's grandfather, as he had in every other dream.

"Because they do not exist!" his son shouted at him. Once again his words echoed across the canyon, but this time they did not cause the horses to fade away. Instead they remained visible and started—all at once—to run. Never before had Wallace heard the sound of a thousand horses running together at the same time. It was like thunder—thunder without a storm.

In his dream, Wallace felt himself shake from the force of their stampede and he saw his grandfather shout something at him, but the sound was too loud for him to hear what he was saying. He looked closely and tried to read his lips as they moved. It looked as though he was telling him to wake up!

He felt his grandfather's arms shaking him awake, and Wallace opened his eyes. He was no longer dreaming, but he could still hear the sound of the thunder.

"Wake up, Wallace!" his grandfather called. "It's here! It's happening! Can you hear it? It's happening."

"The horses?" asked Wallace, confused by what was going on.

"They're here! They've come back!" his grandfather said.

Wallace climbed out of his sleeping bag and the two of them ran out of the tent. Neither of them was fully prepared for what they saw and felt.

The spirits of a thousand horses ran toward them along the red rocks of the canyon.

"Do you see them, Wallace?" asked his grandfather.

"Yes," answered Wallace.

"This is what I was waiting for! This is what I saw with my father all those years ago. Your father wouldn't believe me when I took him here—he thought I was crazy, but I wasn't. They didn't come then, because he refused to believe that they existed, but you believe, don't you?"

Wallace didn't have to say anything. The presence of the horses was enough to confirm the fact that he believed.

Years of playing video games and watching movies with amazing computer-generated special effects had made Wallace jaded to the natural beauty of the world, which often failed to match the marvels of made-up fantasies. But there was no denying that this was the most astonishing and beautiful sight he had ever witnessed.

For a moment he felt afraid as the horses started getting closer and closer to them, but his grandfather assured him that they would be okay. This proved to be true; when the horses approached, they passed through them like they weren't even there. It felt as though they were being engulfed in a warm chinook that was brisk but not at all threatening.

Wallace instinctively reached out for his grandfather's hand. The old man grabbed it, and the two of them stood there together as the ghostly steeds raced through them. The horses ran so fast that it took only a couple of minutes before they were gone and the sound faded away in the distance. They stood there in silence, overcome by the experience they had just shared, before Wallace finally spoke.

"What just happened?" he asked. "What did I just see?"

"Those are the horses of our people," his grandfather explained. "The ones that were slaughtered so that we would never bring any trouble to the white man again. Go restart the fire and I'll tell you the whole story."

Wallace walked over to the pit and built a fire from the embers that were still glowing from the flames that had been blazing just a few hours before. Once the fire was replenished, Wallace sat down and his grandfather started telling him the tale of the thousand Kiowa horses.

*   *   *

"At the end of October 1867, chiefs from the Apache, Comanche, Cheyenne, Arapaho and Kiowa tribes traveled to Medicine Lodge, Kansas, to sign a treaty that they hoped would bring an end to the violence that had been a constant in their lives since the Europeans had arrived in their world. The treaty assigned them reservations of land that they would not have to fight to protect along with payments in the form of supplies and provisions, and it promised to protect their lands from the encroachment of white poachers and liquor traders.

"The chiefs signed the treaty in good faith, assuming its promises were going to be kept, but the men responsible for enforcing its provisions were not honorable. They considered the tribes to be an inconvenient nuisance, and eventually they starved them out of existence.

"The land assigned to the tribes kept getting smaller and smaller and the promised supplies often never arrived, and when they did, never in the quantities that had been agreed upon. But worst of all was the indifference the authorities showed to the activities of the European hunters who trespassed on the tribes' land, hunted their cattle and stole their horses that were so important for their survival. Most often these crimes were completely ignored by the officers assigned to enforce the laws of the treaty, and on the rare occasion that someone was caught and tried, the punishment was so inconsequential that it completely failed to deter them from doing it again.

"After seven years of this treatment, the tribes could no longer allow it to continue. At the end of June 1874, a war party composed of 700 Comanche, Arapaho, Cheyenne and Kiowa warriors descended upon an encampment of white buffalo hunters at Adobe Walls along the Canadian River. Despite their large numbers, they were not as well prepared as the hunters and lost 70 members of their party in the battle.

"A series of similar battles continued throughout that summer. Eventually the American army was able to drive the warriors and their families into the Palo Duro Canyon.

"On September 29, the army, aided by members of the Tonkawa tribe and led by a Colonel Ranald S. Mackenzie, decided to settle the matter once and for all and launched a sneak attack. The tribal villages were too scattered throughout the canyon for the warriors to gather and mount any kind of defense. Villages were destroyed and looted, and the warriors and their families were driven out of the canyon and forced to abandon all of their possessions and return by foot back to their reservations.

"Left behind in the canyon was a herd of 1400 Kiowa horses. Without these horses, the Kiowa people would no longer be able to mount any kind of attack against the American military, or maintain the lifestyle they had lived for centuries. Instead, they would be forced to remain on the increasingly smaller parcel of land doled out to them by the indifferent government that showed no interest in their plight or suffering.

"This suited Colonel Mackenzie just fine.

"After he gave 400 of the horses to the Tonkawa tribe as payment for their help in the attack, he ordered his men to kill the remaining 1000 animals. His men protested—this was an act even they considered too inhumane—but he refused to change his mind.

"As his orders were carried out, the smell of death overtook the canyon, which made even the soldiers retch as they continued their massacre. The sounds of the poor animals' screams could be heard for miles.

"This marked the last time the Comanche, Arapaho, Cheyenne and Kiowa tribes took arms against the government."

*   *   *

"Man, white people suck," Wallace decided after his grandfather finished telling him the story.

"I'm not sure if that is the right conclusion for you to draw from this story," his grandfather told him.

"Really? What else should I think?"

"How about that a lost cause is still worth fighting? Or that no matter what someone takes from you, you can still have your dignity?"

"I dunno," Wallace said. "White people suck still seems to sum it up best."

"Do you really think the spirit of those horses would have visited us for such ignoble a reason?" asked his grandfather.

"No, I guess not," Wallace admitted.

"Then why do you think they came?"

Wallace knew the answer, but he did not want to say it. Tears welled in his eyes as he stared down into the fire.

"You can say it, Wallace," his grandfather said softly, "I will not be offended."

Wallace spoke through his tears, "They came because I was ashamed."

"Ashamed of what?"

"Of being Indian—of being Kiowa, like you."

"Why?"

"Because I thought that was what my dad wanted. He never acknowledged our heritage and I thought it was because it was something to be embarrassed of. But it's not. The horses came to tell me that. They came to tell me that I have every right to be proud of who I am and who my ancestors are. The army may have killed them all, but their deaths' did not stop the Kiowa. You're proof of that and *I'm* proof of that. I acted like such a jerk, and I'm sorry that I didn't want to come here. "

His grandfather smiled. "You're a teenager, I wouldn't have expected you to act any other way. Now let's go back to bed. It's late and we have to get up early tomorrow."

"Okay," said Wallace as he used his arm to wipe away his tears.

*   *   *

Wallace had one more dream that night.

In it, he and his grandfather were both riding on the backs of two phantom horses of the Palo Duro Canyon. Galloping behind them were the other 998 steeds that ran with such force that the ground shook beneath their hooves.

At first Wallace wasn't sure where they were going, but then he saw a small figure of a man standing in the distance. He and his grandfather started riding toward him. It didn't take long for Wallace to recognize it was his father, but not the boy he had seen in his other dreams earlier that week. It was, instead, the man he had grown up with and known all of his life.

It seemed to take a long time to reach him, but when they did—with all of the horses following them—they stopped. Silence followed, which hung in the air like a thick fog.

"Wallace," said his father, breaking the silence. "Are you sure this is what you want?"

"Yes," he said cautiously, afraid that saying so would mean earning his father's disapproval.

"Good," his father answered back. "I am glad to know that you will not repeat the mistake that I made. Be proud of who you are, Wallace. Be proud and never forget."

With that said, Wallace watched his father fade away before waking up.

*   *   *

Wallace did not enjoy the trip back home. Not because it was long and boring—it wasn't—but because it meant that the week was over and he did not know if he would ever have another one like it.

"I suppose you're going to be happy getting back to your Internet and computer games," said his grandfather as they drove in Oklahoma City.

"Yeah," Wallace said half-heartedly.

"What's wrong?" asked the old man, surprised by the boy's lack of enthusiasm.

Once Wallace explained, his grandfather had to fight the urge to smile and managed to stay stoic. "I don't see any reason why we can't go out camping during your summer vacation," he said casually.

"Really?" asked Wallace. "You'd be up for that?"

"I don't see why not."

"Would we go to Palo Duro again?"

"If you want," answered his grandfather, "but if we're going to have the whole summer instead of just a week, we could get a little more ambitious."

"Like how?"

"Well, instead of just going to the Grand Canyon of Texas, it might be fun to go and see the real thing."

"The Grand Canyon?"

"Why not? It is only the most beautiful place in the world."

"Are there any spirits there?"

"I would think there has to be with a place as big and old as that. Does that sound like fun?"

"Yeah."

"Then it's settled."

As they drove back to the city, Wallace was surprised at how he felt inside. It had been so long, but he couldn't remember feeling like this since before his father died.

Wallace was truly happy.

The Empty Village

The following legend is part of the traditional folklore of the Luiseño people who lived along the coast of southern California. Though they lived in autonomous villages, they were united in a common language and way of life. The name Supúlatáax is an amalgam of the Luiseño worlds Supúl (One) and Atáax (Man).

Supúlatáax was a traveler. From a very young age, restlessness constantly ached in his bones and the only way for him to dull the pain was to go on long walks that took him to the neighboring villages. When he was younger his behavior struck many as odd, but as the years passed, it became accepted that he was someone who could not stay in one place for very long. People soon began to look forward to his visits and the stories he brought with him. It was through him that everyone got to hear what was happening in the other villages: how many babies had been born, who had died and other gossip that bonded people together with its sweet familiarity.

Children loved him because he could always be counted on to teach them a new game or tell them an old legend they had never heard before. As he grew older, he became more and more beloved, and eventually his appearance in a village was enough to cause all work to come to a stop, and an instant celebration would begin.

But time takes its toll on everyone and there came a day when Supúlatáax could not travel like he used to. For the first time since anyone could remember, he settled in one village and ceased to roam. His bones still ached with restlessness, but that ache was no match for the pains that came with old age.

His days in Ahoya—the village he had at last decided to call home—were slow and uneventful. He had spent his whole life defeating boredom by going somewhere the moment he felt it strike, but that was no longer an option, and it wasn't long before he started praying that he would soon be allowed to go on the one journey everyone must take in the end.

But time kept passing, and there was no sign that this last journey of his would ever begin. He despaired that he would never be able to take it—he might be cursed to live forever in one place—but then one night a dream came to him as he slept.

In it he saw the village of Kamak, which was not far from Ahoya. He had been there many times in his life and knew that the people there were among the kindest and most generous he had ever known. In his dream they were all dancing to celebrate his return to their village. This was a dream he had had many times since he had stopped traveling, but that night it ended in a way it never had before.

This time, when the dance ended, Supúlatáax lay down on the ground and closed his eyes and, as the villagers covered his body with a large basket, he went on the final journey that had eluded him for so long.

When he awoke from this dream, Supúlatáax was certain that he knew what it meant. Before he could go on his journey into the land of the dead, he would have to travel one last time in the land of the living. He would have to go to Kamak.

Supúlatáax did not think his old bones could handle walking even the short distance between the two villages, but he was far too stubborn not to try. When morning came he got up, dressed in his finest clothes, said goodbye to his friends in Ahoya and started walking toward Kamak.

When he was young it would have taken him just a day to make this journey, but back then he only had to stop and rest a couple of times along the way. Now he had to rest after every couple of steps.

But the weather stayed warm, and it did not rain. When the night arrived, he lay down on the ground and slept until the morning. When he woke up he still had far to travel. The sun would set one more time before he reached the village.

As he walked, he saw many of the sights he had grown so accustomed to seeing when he was young. Having been away for so long, he was able to see them one last time with new eyes. He felt sad for some of the people he knew who had never ventured far from their villages during their entire lives. Their lives would pass without ever seeing the things that he now found so familiar.

His thoughts then drifted to all of the people he would meet again once he reached Kamak. Not just the people who lived there, but all the people he had ever known who were now living in the place the dead call home. It would be good to see them all again—he had missed them and knew that for once they would have stories to tell him, rather than the other way around.

He had moved faster than he thought he would, and it was just turning to dusk. When he walked into the village he waited for all the commotion to begin once he was recognized, but all he heard was silence.

When he reached the center of the village it became clear that it was deserted. It was only then that he realized that this

was the time of year when the people of Kamak would go to
Palomar Mountain to collect acorns. It was such an important event that everyone in the village took part—even the
old and the sick were carried along the way. There was not a
single person left in Kamak to greet Supúlatáax. There was no
one there to celebrate his arrival. His dream had failed him.

But Supúlatáax was very tired. He looked up and saw rain
clouds in the sky, so he would need some sort of shelter. He
needed to rest, but he did not want to enter someone's home
when they were not there. There in the distance was a large
empty grain basket—like the one that had appeared in his
dream. It would have to do. He lay down on the ground and
slipped the basket over his body. The basket was very well
made—the villagers of Kamak were excellent weavers—and
he would not get wet if it rained.

He closed his eyes and fell asleep.

"Come everyone!" The voice was loud and strong and it
startled him awake. "Come everyone and dance! Supúlatáax is
here with us! It is time to dance!"

Supúlatáax's heart leapt with joy when he realized that the
villagers had returned and knew he was there. With an enormous smile on his face, he lifted the large basket off and stood
up. There he found himself surrounded by more people than
he had ever seen together in one place. He recognized them all.

"Supúlatáax's here!" they all shouted together.

And then, at once, everyone began to dance.

Supúlatáax's bones no longer felt any pain—they did not
ache. He cried tears of joy and began to dance.

The entire village celebrated his return.

*   *   *

When the villagers returned from the mountain to Kamak, they were surprised to discover a grain basket in the center of the village. They were even more shocked when they turned it over and found Supúlatáax lying under it.

A smile rested on his face.

His final journey was complete.

The Madness of Mocking Crow

*The Cherokee legend of Nocatula and Connestoga has enter-
tained people for centuries, but never before has the legend been
told from the point of view of its villain, the cruel and jealous
Mocking Crow. Now seems to be a perfect time to do just that.*

It had been so long since Mocking Crow had had a moment's
peace that he had forgotten how long it had been. By our cal-
endar, his misery had endured three and a half decades, while
he had long lost track of time. Days held no meaning for him.
He could not tell the difference between the blue sky of the
day and the dark sky of the night. He only noticed the changing seasons because of the new miseries each season brought
him. In the summer, his body would break out in rashes from
the heat, and in the winter, parts of his body would grow
numb and blue from the cold.

He should have died a very long time ago. Most men, possessed of all their wits, would not survive longer than a few
months living like he did—yet he, a man whose mind was a
fractured wasteland of terror and regret, remained alive, even
as he prayed for death. Living was his curse—each day a fresh
opportunity for the voices in his head to play their games of
torture and torment.

His body was a maze of scars—the result of decades
of rashes, walking bare-skinned through thick brush and

self-flagellation. He was once a strong, handsome man, but you would not know it to look at him. His body was now withered and small, and he walked with a hunch he could no longer correct. His hair hung down his face, hiding his features from the world, which was for the best as few people would have been able to look upon him without screaming.

Mocking Crow had once been a man, but now he was a monster, and on his hip he carried the knife that changed everything; it had not dulled in 35 years. At least once each day, during that time, he pulled it from its leather sheath and held it to his chest, where he could feel it beside the beat of his heart. Each day he would pray for the strength to drive the blade into his body and silence the voices he could not escape any other way.

But the voices could seduce as well as torment, and they would tell him lies before the knife's point pierced his skin. They would tell him that they would torture him no longer, and though he had heard these lies so many times before, he would believe them and put the knife back by his side. Then the torments would continue, just like they had before.

But this day was different, though Mocking Crow had no way of knowing it. To his eyes it was as wretched as any other. It was late autumn and his body trembled in the cold air that surrounded him. The voices continued along in their constant chatter, filling his head with so many thoughts that he could hold on to for only the briefest of seconds.

Then at once, the voices stopped.

The silence was so powerful that it brought Mocking Crow to his knees. It had been so long—he had almost forgotten what quiet was—that it took him a long moment to recognize it.

It was peace.

With tears in his eyes, he grabbed the knife from its torn leather sheath at his side. He placed its point against his chest and again he prayed for the strength to push it through. This time the voices stayed quiet and did not stop him.

He felt such joy as the blade entered his body. For the first time since his journey into madness began, he would finally be freed from his misery.

He was later found lying between two beautiful trees, with a faint smile across his lips.

*   *   *

He was only a small child when his father was killed. Much blood had been spilled that day, but only his father's death came from a blow delivered by one of his own people. He was murdered by the man his tribe called their chief.

It all began with the arrival of the white man—the most treacherous of all creatures. The chief and his people treated them with great respect when they first appeared, but their respect was not returned. The white men did not seem to consider them to be human and felt no duty to honor any of the agreements they had made. They continued to hunt where they swore not to hunt. They continued to trade their intoxicating elixirs for goods, when they said they would not. They were liars and soon even the chief—as blind as he was—came to realize that something had to be done about them.

Mocking Crow's father was overjoyed the day Chief Attakulla-kulla finally decided to declare war on the white man and lay siege on the fortress they called Louden. At last these creatures from the other world would understand that the Cherokee were not to be cheated or ignored—if their people were not to be given the proper respect, then they would take it.

The colonists never saw the attack coming. The chief and his warriors surrounded the white man's fort and kept them trapped inside until they no longer had any food or water and were only days away from dying of thirst. Their leader raised a white flag and asked to speak to Chief Attakulla-kulla. The white man agreed to abandon the fort and leave the land to the Cherokee in exchange for their lives. Like a fool the chief agreed to this deal, but Mocking Crow's father would not be so easily deceived.

"We could not trust them before, why should we trust them now?" he asked his fellow braves. "They say they will go, but we all know that it will only be a matter of time before they come back. And when they do, they will be ready for us and we will not be able to defend ourselves, especially when we are being led by a cowardly fool. He may have agreed to let them live, but I have not and neither have any of you! I say we show them what it feels like to have someone break their word and do as they please. They shall not pass! We shall kill them all!"

Many of the braves were loyal to Attakulla-kulla, who they believed to be a very wise man, and they ignored Mocking Crow's father's call to action, but there were just as many who agreed with what he said and acted accordingly.

To the chief's horror, the braves started attacking the haggard, starving colonists as soon as they started streaming out of the fort.

"Stop this!" Attakulla-kulla shouted at them. "This is not right!" he insisted, but his cries were no match for the cacophony created by the chaos of the sudden attack. The screams of the colonists echoed around the surrounding forest as they were cut down by the mutinous braves.

"Help me!" the chief heard a woman plead in the distance. "Someone please help me! My baby! He's going to kill my baby!"

The chief followed her cries and found a beautiful young woman with a baby in her arms cowering before Mocking Crow's enraged father, who was ready to strike a fatal blow with the weapon he held in his hand.

"Stop!" the chief ordered him.

Mocking Crow's father turned and saw Chief Attakulla-kulla standing before him. "Or what?" he asked his leader. "Will you kill me? Will you kill one of your own people to protect one of our enemies?"

"I gave my word that no harm shall come to them," answered Attakulla-kulla.

"Your word means nothing to them! Why should it mean anything to me?"

"It is a mistake to believe that the crimes of others justify our own," said the chief. "If we act like them, then we are no better than they are and deserve their treachery."

"Only a fool would believe that!"

"Then I am fool. All that matters is that I gave my word to these people and I will do all that I can to keep it, even if it means killing men like you."

"You say those words, but you do not have the courage to enforce them."

"Is that what you really believe, or what you hope is true?"

The two men stared at each other, neither willing to back down. The woman and her baby wept as the tension grew intolerable. Finally, it was Mocking Crow's father who could stand it no more and snapped. With pure rage, he turned to the woman and her child and rose up his weapon to kill her, but before he could strike, Attakulla-kulla struck him down with a single powerful blow.

"You're safe now," the chief told the young woman in her own language. "As long as you are with me, I swear no harm shall come to you."

Later that day when news of what happened between the two men reached their village, it was Mocking Crow's mother who told her son that his father was dead. "Your father was murdered today," she said, "but his death will not be avenged—at least not for now. You are too young to understand, but there will come a time when you will recognize that it is your duty to see that Chief Attakulla-kulla pays a dear price for what he did to us today. Not only has he killed my husband and your father, he did so to protect our enemy. That alone would merit his suffering at our hands, but he has made his crime even worse by bringing this very enemy back to our camp and treating her and her foul child as honored guests. This can never be forgiven."

In the end Chief Attakulla-kulla did more than just take in the white woman as his guest—he made her his wife and adopted her young son. Though she said nothing, this escalated Mocking Crow's mother's fury to a murderous level of rage. He was never able to confirm it, but Mocking Crow believed that when the baby died not long after the marriage, it was his mother who killed him.

As for the chief's new bride, nature took her before his mother could. She died giving birth to the chief's only child, a girl he named Nocatula. Mocking Crow was sure this child would have met the same fate as the last, if his mother had not died before her chance for vengeance.

His mother's death was also a mystery. She was found lying cold on the ground without a single mark on her body.

204 Native American Ghost Stories

Some said that she had succumbed to the grief that had never left her following her husband's death, but Mocking Crow believed that, like his father, she was murdered by Attakulla-kulla, as retaliation for the death of his adopted baby son.

Those who had the chief's ear advised Attakulla-kulla to banish the orphaned Mocking Crow from the village, because they feared what he would do once he became a man. They knew that a boy his age would never be able to survive out in the wilderness alone, but they felt it had to be done to ensure the continued peace of the village.

Attakulla-kulla, however, refused to listen to them. What he did instead shocked almost everyone. He declared that he would raise Mocking Crow as his son. "I am, in part, responsible for what has happened to this child," he explained. "I am obligated to protect him, not cast him aside for what he might or might not do in the future. If, in time, he decides to wreak havoc on our tribe, I will take action against him then, but not before."

The chief believed that Mocking Crow was still young enough to forget about the fate of his parents. He hoped that someday the young boy would come to consider him his true father, but that day never came. Mocking Crow never forgot what his adoptive father had done to his family, and he vowed to never let the chief's kindness deter him from someday getting his revenge.

*   *   *

Over the course of the years, there was only one person who could have softened Mocking Crow's resolve to destroy Attakulla-kulla: his adopted sister, Nocatula.

Even as a small child, Nocatula's beauty was startling to behold, and it only grew more powerful and bewitching once she became a young woman. She was loved and adored by everyone in the village, and she managed to return the affection she received in a way that made people feel special.

Of all her many admirers, it was only her adopted brother whom she treated with anything that resembled contempt. Though she tried hard not to, she had grown to dislike him because of his obvious hatred for her father and because his devotion to her had more to do with an obvious obsession than with any sort of love.

"Someday I am going to marry her," he once told his good friend, Cunning Fox, who was, ironically, one of the dumbest men in the village.

"But she is your sister," said Cunning Fox. "A brother cannot marry his sister, no matter how beautiful she is."

"I am not her brother," Mocking Crow said boldly. "That old fool may have taken me as his son, but I am no more a part of his family than you are."

"He's my uncle," Cunning Fox reminded him.

"See," Mocking Crow replied, "you are more a part of his family than I am. I share none of their blood, so I see no reason why I cannot take Nocatula as my wife."

"But she doesn't like you. In fact, she hates you. The only time she ever frowns is when you are near her. I have actually seen her shudder when you have touched her."

"Don't be a fool, Cunning Fox," Mocking Crow ordered his friend. "She is just pretending when she acts like that. I know she loves me as much as I do her, but she cannot show it or else she will get in trouble with her father."

"If she is pretending, then she is very good at it. She has convinced everyone in the village, except you."

*   *   *

In order to prove himself worthy of the love of the village's most prized beauty, Mocking Crow dedicated himself to becoming a skilled brave. His feats of bravery earned him many admirers. Had he not been so obsessed with marrying Nocatula, he could have had any of the other young women in the village as his wife. Like his father, he earned a following among the other braves, but he was not yet strong enough to overthrow the chief.

He constantly fought with Attakulla-kulla about what to do about the white men, who were now embroiled in a war among themselves. It would only be a matter of time before the violence at Fort Louden was forgotten and more settlers would return. Mocking Crow wanted his adopted father to discourage these people by killing all white men who ventured into Cherokee territory, but the old fool refused to listen to him.

"If we declare war on all white men," Attakulla-kulla told him, "it will mean the end of us. The people at Fort Louden were not prepared for our attack—that is why we are able to defeat them. But we would be no match for an army that was expecting us."

"We can defeat any army we face!" Mocking Crow insisted. "We are the strongest and bravest people in the world!"

"It does my heart proud to hear you say that, but you are young and do not know the dangers that can come from underestimating your enemy. It is for our own good that we maintain a peaceful existence with these people. For all we know they will soon wipe each other out in their own war, and we will not have to worry about them any longer."

Mocking Crow stayed silent. He would not argue with his chief any longer, but that did not mean he would do as the old man said.

*   *   *

Everyone in the village was awoken one morning by the sound of exploding gunpowder in the distance. The white man's war was getting closer to them. It would only be a matter of time before it directly intruded into their lives. In fact, it would only be a few hours.

Intrigued by the potential sight of hundreds of white men killing each other, Mocking Crow decided to go into the forest and travel toward the sound of the skirmish. As he walked he grew disappointed when the sounds of war began to fade, suggesting that the battle was over. Still, he continued forward, assuming he would at least have the chance to see a field strewn with bloody corpses.

It turned out that he didn't have to go that far to see such a sight.

At the edge of a small, hidden clearing in the woods, he found the body of a white soldier in the red and white uniform of the side fighting for their king across the ocean. Mocking Crow smiled and walked toward the body and bent down for a better look. As he did, the soldier involuntarily sputtered out a mouthful of blood, some of which splattered across Mocking Crow's face.

Enraged, Mocking Crow grabbed his knife at his side and was about to slash the man's throat, when he was stopped by a voice behind him.

"Put that knife down!" it ordered him.

Mocking Crow sneered and turned to see who would dare stop him from killing this creature at his feet. It was Nocatula.

"What do you think you're doing?" she asked.

"What has to be done," he answered, snarling at her, with his knife aimed at the man's throat.

"I said put that knife down," she said again.

"Or else what? You'll tell your father?"

"Yes."

"Go ahead! I do not fear him!"

"Not yet," she said, "but that is only because he does not know of the things you have said to me in the past about love and marriage. If I were to tell him, I believe that his response would terrify even someone as brave as you."

Mocking Crow glared at her, but he knew she was right. If Attakulla-kulla found out about his desire for Nocatula, he would banish him from the village forever. "Have it your way," he told her as he returned his knife to its leather sheath. "All you are doing is prolonging his misery. I would have given him a quick, merciful death, but I will allow you to let him suffer."

"Thank you for your generosity," she said to him coldly.

He glared at her as he stood up and left the clearing. As he walked, Nocatula turned and shouted for help from the village. She could always get to the full attention of every available man, and it didn't take long for help to arrive to take the wounded soldier back to the village.

*   *   *

The soldier did not die. Nocatula stayed with him day and night as she tended to his wounds. When he was well enough to speak, Chief Attakulla-kulla came and talked to him, informing him where he was and that he was welcome to stay as their guest as long as his health required.

Mocking Crow fumed at the thought of the village once again serving as host to one of the people whose race was indirectly responsible for the destruction of his family. He grew angrier as he observed the chief spending more time with the soldier, whose name was John. His imagination went to very dark places as he contemplated what the two men could be talking about. Was Attakulla-kulla conspiring with the white man? Was he working on a plan to betray his people for his own benefit?

He shared these concerns with some of his friends, but even they could not believe that the old man would do such a thing. Though they shared Mocking Crow's disrespect for Attakulla-kulla, it was inconceivable to them that he could ever be any kind of traitor to his people.

But as concerned as he was about the presence of the white man and his meetings with his adoptive father, what really enraged Mocking Crow about this situation was the devotion Nocatula showed to the wounded soldier. He no longer labored under the delusion that she merely pretended to dislike her—he now knew her antipathy was very real, and he could not stomach the thought that she would rather spend nearly all of her time tending to the needs of the dying white man than spend even one moment with him.

But this knowledge did nothing to lessen his desire to someday call her his wife—if anything that desire was stronger now than it ever had been before. The difference was that now he did not want her because he loved her, but because he wanted no other man to have her.

If he could not marry Nocatula, then no man would.

*   *   *

Much time had passed. The soldier was close to being fully recovered, and it had been revealed that his meetings with the old man were spent with him learning their language, so he could speak with the beautiful woman who saved his life. Mocking Crow had not spoken to Nocatula since he had held a knife to that white man's neck, but not for a lack of trying on his part.

He eventually got his chance when he cornered her outside the hut in which John was convalescing.

"How is your white man today?" he asked her.

"He is well, Mocking Crow," she answered curtly.

"He would not be if it had been up to me."

"You do not have to remind me. Yours has never been a generous heart."

"What has he done to deserve our kindness and mercy?"

"Our kindness and mercy, Mocking Crow? The last time you had anything to do with him your blade was ready to cut his throat!"

"What has he done to deserve all of *your* time caring for him?"

"Nothing," she answered defiantly, "but I would not want to imagine a world where I only help people that you believe are deserving of our generosity."

"Why do you hate me?" Mocking Crow asked, surprising even himself with his directness.

"I don't think you could stand to hear all of the reasons," she said. "There is your arrogance, your cruelty, your lack of gratitude for the man who saved your life, but most of all, there is the coldness that has frozen your heart and made it impossible for you to feel anything but hatred and fear."

"If I am that way, it is because of your father."

"No," said Nocatula. "You cannot blame who you are on him. If he had listened to the people around him, you would not be here now. They were prepared to show you the same level of mercy you showed to John, but he ignored them all and adopted you as his own. And how do you repay back his kindness? By proving that those who would have banished you from the village were right all along. You could have chosen to become a good man, but you didn't, and for that you have only yourself to blame."

At that moment Mocking Crow wanted to strike her as hard as he could, but he did not. Without a word, he turned away from her.

"You chose to be who you are!" she shouted after him. "But that doesn't mean you can't choose a better path."

*   *   *

Not long after that came the day when John was able to leave the hut and walk around the village. With Nocatula on his arm, helping him stay on his feet, it didn't take him long to make new friends. It also didn't take him long to make new enemies.

"Can you believe how she insults us by parading him around like that?" Cunning Fox asked his friends.

"My sister heard her tell someone that she is in love with him," said Glowing Ember. "I think she wants to marry him."

"We cannot allow that to happen," insisted Dark Storm.

All three of them looked over to the man they considered their leader.

"No," agreed Mocking Crow, "we won't."

*   *   *

Chief Attakulla-kulla gathered the people of the village together so he could tell them the good news.

"Since he first came to our village, I have been lucky to get to know our guest who goes by the name of John. Though I could talk to him in his language, he requested that I teach him our own, so he could talk to us all. This was the first indication I received that he was a good man. The second was the speed with which he learned our tongue, although I suspect that his desire to speak with someone in particular helped him a great deal. And the third came when my daughter told me that she loved him. I know Nocatula better than anyone else in the world and I believe she is incapable of loving a man who would be unworthy of her. That is why, when John asked me yesterday if he could make her his wife, I told him he could."

Many people cheered when they heard this news, but their celebration was drowned out by the shouts of protest that came from Mocking Crow and his friends.

"How can you call yourself Chief when you would allow your daughter to marry a white man?" shouted Cunning Fox.

"Are we supposed to accept that one of her own people is not good enough for her?" asked Dark Storm.

"Admit that this is part of your plot to betray us to your white masters!" ordered Glowing Ember.

Chief Attakulla-kulla's face filled with rage as he listened to these questions and accusations. He looked at his adopted son, knowing that he had to be source behind these voices of dissent. "Have you nothing to say, Mocking Crow?" he asked angrily.

"I do not have to, when your actions provide all of the answers I need. You are a traitor to our people and everyone knows it!" Mocking Crow shouted.

The chief's people raised their voices to show that they did not agree with him.

"I had hoped," Chief Attakulla-kulla said sadly, "that you would not grow up to be like your father."

"A great man!" shouted Cunning Fox.

"Who you killed to protect a white woman and her child!" added Glowing Ember.

The chief ignored them and continued. "You cannot know the sadness I feel at this moment, but I see at last that we cannot continue with you around to spread your poison throughout the village. You have left me no choice, Mocking Crow. From this moment on you are banished from this village and are never to return. If you do, it will mean your death. The same goes for Cunning Fox, Glowing Ember and Dark Storm, who have become as corrupted as you are by your hate. I hope the four of you will find some happiness on the hard path that you have chosen for yourselves."

"Chosen!" screamed Mocking Crow. "I never chose to have you kill my father! I never chose to have you pretend to be my father!"

"Enough!" ordered the chief. "Leave now or suffer the ultimate consequence!"

The four banished men looked at each other and decided at that moment to do what they were told, but they all knew that this was not over.

*   *   *

The next day, Nocatula and John were married. During the ceremony John was made an official member of the tribe and given the new name of Connestoga. He and his new wife were the happiest couple in the village and everyone knew it.

But their happiness proved to be short lived.

Not long after they were married, Connestoga went out into the woods to hunt for food. He wasn't gone for long when he felt a hand grab his right shoulder. He turned and saw the smiling face of Mocking Crow standing in front of him.

"We have never actually met, have we, white man?" the banished brave asked Nocatula's husband. "The last time I was this close to you, I had my blade pressed against your throat."

"You'll have to forgive me for not remembering that," Connestoga said coolly. He started to reach for his knife, but before he could get to it, Mocking Crow's three cohorts grabbed him from behind. One of them hit him over the head with something heavy and he fell to the ground in an unconscious heap.

They took him to their makeshift camp, tied him up and left him there as they continued on the second part of their mission, which required that they wait for nightfall and sneak into the village so that they could take what should have been Mocking Crow's all along. They had hoped that Nocatula would be asleep when they arrived, but she was too worried about her husband's absence to rest that evening.

Nocatula started to scream when she saw them, but Glowing Ember was able to silence her with a blow to the head, as he did with Connestoga. They then carried her back to their camp and tied her up beside her husband.

Mocking Crow waited for the morning to arrive. He wanted the sun to be in the sky, so his adopted sister could see everything that he did to her husband. "Wake up!" he ordered, with a shout that served as tribute to his name.

Both of them responded to his command by slowly opening their eyes.

"Mocking Crow," said Nocatula, "what do you think you're doing?"

"What I should have done in the first place, *sister*. You and your father both have faulted me for the choices I have made, but I can only think of one that I regret and that was not slashing the throat of this creature you call your husband. Thankfully, this is a mistake I won't make again."

Nocatula began to scream as Mocking Crow unsheathed his knife and used it to cut her husband's throat. Before her eyes, Connestoga bled to death, unable to say a single word of farewell. As he died, she stopped screaming and the two of them stared into each other's eyes until it was clear that he was no longer there.

"There," said Mocking Crow, "now you are free to become what you were always meant to be."

"If you think I will ever become your wife, then you are even more insane than I ever could have imagined. Know this, Mocking Crow, you shall be punished for what you have done today."

"I'm not afraid of your father!"

"I am not talking about my father!" she shouted back at him. "You are going to be punished by forces far greater than Attakulla-kulla."

"What forces?"

"The spirits of the man and the woman whom you captured and killed because you could not bear the thought of their love. They will torture you and taunt you for the rest of your life, which will last far longer than any man could possibly endure."

Mocking Crow laughed at her. "If I planned to kill you, I would not be able to make you my wife. How can your spirit torture me when you are not dead?"

"Exactly," said Nocatula, as she threw herself at him.

It happened too fast for Mocking Crow to get out of the way. She hurled herself at him and in an instant the knife in his hand stabbed her directly in her heart.

She died instantly.

*   *   *

Dark Storm, Cunning Fox and Glowing Ember got off easily for their crimes. They were found by Chief Attakulla-kulla and his braves and executed on the spot. Mocking Crow would not be so lucky; he escaped.

True to her word, the spirits of his adopted sister and her husband taunted and tortured him night and day. Thirty-five years passed and each day he tried to end his own life, but could not. It was only when he found himself standing in front of those two beautiful trees did the spirits leave him and allow him to end his life.

Mocking Crow did not know where he was or the significance of those mighty oaks. It was the spot where he had murdered Nocatula and Connestoga all those years ago. It was where her father and his braves found their bodies, and where they were buried. To mark their graves Attakulla-kulla placed an acorn in Connestoga's hand and a hackberry seed in his daughter's. The seeds grew into the beautiful trees that served as markers of their final resting place.

In the years that followed Mocking Crow's death, many people believed that it was the spirits of Nocatula and Connestoga that had tortured Mocking Crow for all those years. The spirits had possessed the trees that marked their graves, and there they stayed until the trees were finally cut down many years later.

The End